THE
FUTURE
of
WAR
CRIMES
JUSTICE

THE FUTURE of WAR CRIMES JUSTICE

Chris Stephen

MELVILLE HOUSE UK
LONDON

THE FUTURE of WAR CRIMES JUSTICE

First published in 2024 by
Melville House UK
Suite 2000
16/18 Woodford Road
London E7 0HA

and

Melville House Publishing
46 John Street
Brooklyn, NY 11200I

mhpbooks.com @melvillehouse

A CIP catalogue record for this book is available from the British Library

ISBN: 978-1-911545-65-1

1 3 5 7 9 10 8 6 4 2

Printed in Denmark by Nørhaven, Viborg
Typesetting by Roland Codd

The Shock

*'I have no adequate terms with which to depict
to your majesty the brutal acts of your soldiers.'*
George Washington Williams, Stanley Falls, July 1890

Early on the morning of 24 February 2022, Russian
forces fired a Tochka missile from a launcher deployed
in the flat mist-covered fields of eastern Ukraine.

The top of the Tochka missile held a 9N123K
cluster munition warhead. That warhead is made up
of fifty grey metal cylinders, each the size and shape
of a small water bottle. They are filled with explosive
and eighteen rings are scored around the cylinder.
Those rings ensure that when the explosive is triggered, the cylinder tears along the lines, producing
dozens of pieces of jagged steel shrapnel. If the warhead explodes as intended, the hot shrapnel is fired
in a wide arc approaching the speed of sound. That
gives the shrapnel the power to penetrate metal,
wood or flesh with ease. The munition is designed

to clear enemy troops and vehicles from a wide area. But this particular munition was aimed at a hospital.

The missile arced into the hospital, in the small town of Vuhledar, exploding without warning in the car park close to the main building. The cluster munitions detonated as they were designed to do, and ripped through the bodies of fourteen civilians who happened to be around the car park at the time. Four were torn to pieces, another ten grievously wounded. The surprise was all the greater for the victims because Russia had launched its invasion of Ukraine only a few hours before.

That incident alone would have been enough to trigger a war crimes investigation of Russia's invasion. But it was not alone. There were three more missile strikes on civilian targets that day. And thousands more in the days that followed.

Barely a month into the war, the chief prosecutor of the International Criminal Court (ICC) opened a war crimes investigation. And, just over a year after that, he charged Russia's president with war crimes.

Vladimir Putin is the most powerful person ever to be charged with war crimes. In fact, he is the most powerful kind of person who *can* be charged with war crimes. Not just the president of a nuclear-armed former superpower, but the head of a state that is one of the permanent five members of the UN Security Council. For the ICC, it was as if the Nuremberg trials had indicted Hitler. Modern war crimes justice had claimed its greatest scalp.

Claimed, but not taken possession. As dramatic as Putin's indictment was, he will almost certainly never stand trial. The International Criminal Court is not universal. It covers only states that agree that it can judge them. That is about two thirds of all the countries in the world. But many of the worst war crimes take place in the other third. Putin can be charged because Ukraine recognises the court, but he cannot be arrested because Russia does not. Barring an unlikely voluntary surrender of their president by Russia, the most important war crimes suspect of all time will go free.

That is the grim reality for a war crimes court already in trouble. The International Criminal Court is the first permanent war crimes court in history. But in its first twenty years, it has jailed just five war criminals. Meanwhile, wars and war crimes continue to rage around the world.

As things stand, the ICC's future may be the same as its present. It will make a dent on some war crimes in some wars, but will remain a peripheral force. Summed up as a nice idea which didn't work.

❘ ❭ ❭ ▸ ▶ ▶

This book explores what needs to happen if war crimes justice is to change the game. I am not a lawyer but a journalist, my experience of war crimes derived from reporting on nine conflicts for *The Guardian* and other newspapers. I saw war crimes justice from the inside after being asked to be a witness in the case of a Bosnian commander accused of responsibility for numerous crimes. The atrocities were very real, but were committed by a militia the commander had been battling against. As far as I could see, it made no sense to charge him with crimes he had been trying to prevent and I agreed to provide evidence for the defence. In the event, he died of natural causes before the trial, so I never got my turn in the witness box. What I did get, from meeting his lawyers, was an understanding of the possibilities of war crimes justice. I later wrote a book charting the creation of the first war crimes courts and their most high-profile trial, that of former Serbian president Slobodan Milošević.

In the text that follows I have avoided, wherever possible, legalistic terminology. Not because I have anything against lawyers, but because war crimes justice needs to be understood by all, not just its practitioners.

The Putin Problem

The prosecution of Vladimir Putin is easy. Easy, in the sense that the collision of three hurricanes is the 'perfect' storm. It is easy because the two obstacles that confront most war crimes cases are easy to surmount in the Putin case.

War crimes trials are two trials in one. First, the crimes themselves, out on the battlefield. The missile slamming into a hospital; murder and torture. The second trial is working up the chain of command to the boss. In complexity and expense, it is like one of the anti-Mafia prosecutions in Italy or the United States. Many trigger-pullers, many crimes, many bosses.

In most of the short history of war crimes trials, proving both the crimes *and* the chain of command to the top are a problem. Finding the trigger-pullers means sifting mass graves and locating survivors. The chain of command is equally difficult to establish because few commanders order war crimes in writing. And, in much of the world, a commander has no formal position, and there is no easy way to tie them to crimes of subordinates. Neither is a problem with the Putin case.

A day after the Vuhledar hospital missile attack, detailed reports were published by Amnesty International and Human Rights Watch. Unlike most wars, investigators were on the ground to watch crimes as they happened. The problem was not shortage of evidence, but the huge quantity of it.

Putin announced that the Ukraine invasion was a 'special military operation' and would last a few days. Ukrainian resistance, and weapons from Nato, wrecked that timetable. Russia's forces were too poorly equipped and too few in number for the multiple axes of advance of the invasion. In late March, Russian forces abandoned their attempt to encircle the capital, Kyiv, and retreated to the Belarusian border. Ukrainian forces surged into the vacated territory and found new horrors. In Bucha, a suburb of Kyiv, the bodies of 419 civilians killed by various weapons were found. Dozens had their hands tied behind their backs, killed with a bullet to the head.

A torture chamber was uncovered in a basement, where mutilated bodies were discovered. Survivors emerged from the ruins to tell investigators, from the ICC and from Ukraine itself, about torture and beatings. Women and teenaged girls reported being gang-raped by soldiers. Crucially, investigators were able to identify the Russian units involved. The evidence came from witnesses and signals intercepts, but also from more unlikely sources: cellphones found on the bodies of dead soldiers, discarded uniforms, identification panels on smashed tanks, graffiti on the walls and intercepted text messages from the soldiers themselves.

Positively identifying the units, and often the soldiers, who had committed the crimes made the second part of the case equally easy. Evidence for a chain of command stretching to the Kremlin was provided by Russia itself. Article 87 of the Russian constitution specifies that the president is commander-in-chief of the armed forces. That makes him responsible for what those forces do. The president issues orders to a security council of senior generals responsible for carrying out his wishes. In lay terms, that makes Putin's indictment an open-and-shut case.

Aiming for the top is key in war crimes prosecutions. That is based on a simple logic. If you charge only the trigger-pullers, that leaves a warlord free to recruit more trigger-pullers. The only surprise, when Putin was indicted, was the choice of crime. The bombs and missiles, massacres, rape and torture were ignored. Instead he was charged with just one crime – the deportation of Ukrainian children.

At face value, ignoring all the other crimes makes no sense. But it makes sense politically.

The ICC's chief prosecutor, Britain's Karim Khan, who has long war crimes experience, was a bold choice to lead the court. He is the first ICC chief prosecutor to have made his name defending, not prosecuting, war criminals. Among his former clients are Liberia's Charles Taylor, jailed for horrors in Sierra Leone so extensive that the term 'blood diamonds' was coined to describe them. He worked also to defend Saif Gaddafi, son of the former Libyan dictator. Khan lost both cases: Taylor was jailed and Gaddafi remains indicted, and officially on the run. But Khan drew admiration for working with what he had. Charging Putin with child abduction appeared designed to highlight one of the most perverse of crimes.

First, the crime is particularly abhorrent. Ukraine says more than a thousand children were captured from occupied territory, then sent back to Russia.

What happened to them is no secret: Putin himself boasted about it. They were distributed among Russian families, to be adopted as their own. He is jointly charged with Maria Lvova-Belova, the presidential commissioner for children's rights. Far from hiding it, both were filmed by Russian television boasting of the programme. In lay terms, prosecutors see it as the equivalent of bank robbers filming themselves robbing the bank.

The charge was issued with an eye on Russia's remaining allies. Those allies might dismiss war crimes charges for massacres and bombardment as the inevitable detritus of war, but child abduction is something uniquely detestable. Nobody wants to be pictured shaking hands with a child abductor.

With this choice of charge, Khan highlighted that war crimes justice is not just about punishment, but prevention. The dead cannot be brought back to life, but captured children can be returned. Within a week of the charge being filed, Russia began sending some of the captured children home.

It is unlikely, either, to be the only indictment. Khan is free to add more charges later. Moscow knows he may already have done so, in so-called sealed warrants, which are secret indictments. That should be worrying all officials involved in the child abduction. The significance, likely not lost on the Kremlin, is that Khan was unafraid to indict the top man. Moscow may have been hoping that the year's delay in issuing charges for the Ukraine invasion meant the court was nervous. By contrast, it took just three months for the ICC to charge Muammar Gaddafi with war crimes. Charging the president of a nuclear-armed power carries political risks, and military ones too. Days after the charges were announced, Moscow officials told television interviewers they planned on targeting the Hague courthouse with the same missiles being fired at Ukraine.

Yet the reality is that no matter how many charges are attached to Putin, there is nothing to compel him to come to trial. Despite its name, the ICC is not a world court. Rather, it works like a private members' club. States join it, and collectively govern it. They all agree to be judged by the court. A total of 123 nations have joined the court and Ukraine is among those non-members who give it jurisdiction. That means any war crimes on its territory can be investigated, no matter who commits them. But finding a way to bring Russians to trial is something else. This is all the more frustrating for prosecutors at The Hague, because they know if Putin does appear in the dock, most of the defences he might hope to use will fail.

Starting with the defence of necessity. The law says there is never an excuse for war crimes. And that precedent has a long history. It is a precedent taught in law schools around the world, and a vivid one.

In 1884, a cabin boy named Richard Parker was shipwrecked along with three crewmen. They jumped into a lifeboat in the Atlantic and drifted for three weeks. Facing starvation, the three older crewmen decided they had no choice but to kill and eat Parker. Later rescued, two of them confessed to having done it, thinking that what happened at sea stayed at sea.

Wrong, said a court in the English city of Exeter. In a ruling that has echoed down the years, the judges concluded that there is never a good reason for murder. War crimes law follows the same logic. A crime is a crime, no matter the circumstances.

Nor can Putin, or his co-accused, say they were following orders. That defence went out at Nuremberg, the trials of Nazis held after the Second World War. Putin is anyway cast in the role of the person giving the orders, but his generals would get no protection by claiming they were only following those orders. In law, an order to commit war crimes is illegal. The consequence is that following such an order is illegal too.

Putin might argue that the war crimes, if not necessary, were out of his hands. He had no choice but to let them happen. That too is no defence. The precedent was one of the very first modern war crimes convictions. In 1996 a former soldier in Bosnia, Dražen Erdemović, came forward and confessed he had been part of the Srebrenica massacre. Serb forces had stormed the Bosnian town in 1995, then rounded up and slaughtered more than seven thousand men and boys. It was the biggest single massacre in Europe since the Second World War. Erdemović told the judges he was confessing because he was wracked with guilt. He described being given a machine gun and told to mow down captives lined up in front of him. But, he said, he had no choice. If he had not killed the prisoners, his commanders would have shot him.

Too bad, said the judges. In law, you always have a choice. Not always a good choice, and in Erdemović's case, a terrible one of kill or be killed. In law, a crime is a crime. In the event, Erdemović was given a reduced sentence because he had turned himself in. Until he came forward, Hague prosecutors had never heard of him.

Putin would also fail with the argument that the ICC has no jurisdiction because Russia is not a member. All crimes on Ukrainian territory are under ICC jurisdiction, whoever commits them.

Neither is ignorance of the law an excuse. Laws apply, whether you know them or not. A British driver renting a car in Florida and driving the wrong way down the highway won't escape getting a ticket for not knowing Americans drive on the right.

Alternatively, Putin could claim ignorance not of the law, but of the fact that his units were committing war crimes. After all, he wasn't there, wasn't even in the same country. It is one of the main defences put up in war crimes trials around the world. And it is invalid because of a sometimes controversial facet of war law, which says a commander can be guilty even if they didn't know. A commander is deemed responsible for their units. And for knowing what they do.

Command responsibility is one of the bedrocks of war law. It says, loosely, that if troops do the crime, the commander does the time. That doesn't apply to all crimes. Isolated incidents are allowed, an acknowledgement that crimes happen in war, as they do in peace. The test is whether these atrocities are widespread. If they are, a commander has a duty to know about them.

The one defence where Putin might hope to get traction is immunity. Customary international law decrees that presidents and government ministers have immunity from arrest. But customary law is just that. There is no universally agreed law book on immunity. And for the ICC, if they get you to trial, that trial proceeds.

But getting Putin to trial is not easy, even if he visits foreign countries. ICC member states have an obligation to arrest him. But they also have other obligations. In contrast to the ICC, the UN's International Court of Justice (ICJ) has ruled that ministers cannot be arrested while they are ministers. So, Putin will hope that a state he visits decides it cannot, after all, hand him in. Complicating things still further is the way immunity works. The immunity the ICJ insists ministers have is conditional. They cannot be arrested, but only while they hold office. Once they cease holding office, they can be detained for crimes committed while in office. Some high officials have found that out the hard way. In the 1950s, Egypt's King Farouk refused to pay Christian Dior for expensive dresses he bought for his wife in Paris, claiming sovereign immunity to prevent him being sued. But after he was deposed in 1952, that immunity ended, and a French court ruled he had to pay damages to Dior for those dresses. His immunity no longer counted.

What all this means is there is no one agreed rule on immunity. Even diplomatic immunity is complicated.

Under the Vienna Convention, a diplomat cannot be arrested for any reason. But it is the hosting country that decides to accredit diplomats. The notion of being able to travel the world on a diplomatic passport in order to gain immunity is false. Putin is the fourth president the ICC has charged with war crimes, and its rule is simple: if you are brought to court, you go on trial. The nearest the world has come to a test case of the conflicting versions of immunity was in South Africa in 2017. When Sudan's president Omar al-Bashir paid a state visit, South Africa's highest court ruled that under ICC law he had no immunity and must be arrested. In the event, the South African government simply ignored the court ruling and allowed al-Bashir to fly away. All of which means Putin will take a chance if he travels to an ICC-affiliated state. Legally, the state must arrest him, but its government may choose not to.

If, however, Putin does end up in The Hague, he will not be able to free himself by claiming wrongful arrest. That particular issue was dramatically exposed in 1961 in one of the most explosive war crimes trials in history, that of Adolf Eichmann.

Eichmann was, if not the architect of the Holocaust, then certainly the man who organised it. When Israel discovered him living in Argentina after the war, one option was to assassinate him. Instead, the authorities decreed he be brought to trial. A commando team infiltrated Argentina, captured and drugged him, and smuggled him to Israel on a civilian airliner.

Eichmann had grounds to protest he had been the victim of a kidnapping. And so he had, judges would likely have ruled. Except that the issue of how he came to the trial was a separate matter. For the judges, the fact was that he was in court, and would answer for his crimes.

'Innocent until proven guilty' is more than a slogan for the International Criminal Court. The bane of the lives of its press officers are media reports calling suspects 'indicted war criminals'. No, they remind the journalists, unless they are convicted they are only suspects. This principle is as central as the court's demand that guilt be proved beyond reasonable doubt. Nevertheless, prosecutors will be confident that if they bring Putin to court, they will get a conviction.

That is dampened by the realisation that barring a freak event, Putin will never come to The Hague. His trial will not rescue the ICC from its current lethargy, highlighted by its lack of convictions. Many are shocked to discover that a court that has spent three billion dollars over two decades can end up jailing just five war criminals.

The fact that the ICC cannot investigate the third of the world where many war crimes take place, notably Iraq, Myanmar and Yemen, is only one reason for its lack of success. It is also because of failures closer to home. Prosecutors have presided over a long string of blunders, often caustically referenced by judges at The Hague. They have been condemned for concealing evidence, failing to conceal the identities of protected witnesses, failing to disclose necessary facts to the defence and using unreliable freelance investigators in place of their own staff. There have been a chain of embarrassing high-profile acquittals, notably of Kenya's president, Uhuru Kenyatta. He was accused of responsibility for the deaths of 1,200 people in post-election violence, but the case collapsed amid claims that witnesses on whom prosecutors were relying had been intimidated or bribed into silence. The court is also hamstrung by its budget. $150 million may sound a lot, but only about $90 million reaches the prosecutors, and must currently be spread among cases in fourteen separate states. Reports from The Hague speak of Khan having brought new focus and discipline to the prosecution department, taking only cases where evidence is strong. Time, and the conviction rate, will show if that is working. What is clear is that for the ICC to be more effective, it needs the same drive and imagination as the people who invented war law in the first place.

The Pioneers

The Battle of Solferino in 1859 was the biggest military engagement in Europe since Waterloo forty-four years before. Two armies, totalling 300,000 troops, faced each other in two parallel lines stretching more than twenty kilometres. On one side was Austria, occupier of that part of Italy, led by its emperor Franz Joseph. On the other was France, augmented by forces from Piedmont, fighting for Italian independence. They were led by Emperor Napoleon III, nephew of his more famous namesake. Napoleon saw himself as champion of Italian freedom, though a British prime minister described him as 'creating as much mischief as there are rabbits in a warren'. The battle was as simple as it was bloody. At dawn, Napoleon's forces attacked, and by late afternoon the battered Austrian line was broken. The Austrians retreated eastwards with Napoleon's army in pursuit. Behind them they left 16,000 dead and another 22,000 wounded. What army medical services there were had marched off with their armies. The walking wounded headed for a little town named Castiglione which had been at the centre of the fight.

By evening the streets were full of wounded men begging for water after a day out in the burning heat. Into this tumult came a horse-drawn carriage, which stopped in the main square. Out of it stepped a man in a white suit. His name was Henry Dunant. He was neither a doctor nor a soldier, but an impulsive thirty-one-year-old Swiss businessman.

Dunant was there by chance. He had no interest in the war, only in making contact with Napoleon. His problem was that he was the manager of a new farming estate in French-occupied Algeria. The estate was facing ruin because the authorities refused to give the farmers access to water from two rivers. Dunant's plan was to meet Napoleon and convince him to write him a letter supporting the farm. That, he was sure, would convince the authorities to give him his water. In his quest, he had followed Napoleon's path into Italy. But what he saw that night changed his outlook, and changed history.

Dunant was a born organiser, but not always a successful one. He had a history of forming organisations with altruistic purposes. Among them, in his native Geneva, were the Thursday Association, a bible study club, and the Geneva chapter of the YMCA. That night in Castiglione he plunged into the task of organising help for the wounded. First, he sent his carriage west, telling his driver to buy all the medical supplies he could find in neighbouring towns. Next, he marshalled the townspeople into organising a human bucket chain to carry water from the nearest river to the wounded. He found the town's priest and persuaded him to open the church to the wounded, advising they be laid out in lines along the floor. Walking down the lines of wounded men inside, lit by candlelight, he recorded how their faces turned to follow him like sunflowers.

For three days he stayed at Castiglione, helping bring order to the chaos. How much of the good ministries to the wounded were his doing, and how much the population did anyway, is unclear. What is clear is that the experience changed his life. Or anyway, after he finally caught up with Napoleon, and was given a firm 'no' on gaining support for his water project.

Back in Geneva, he wrote a book about his experiences at Solferino, and used it to lobby for a new kind of medical organisation. It would be staffed by doctors and nurses and deploy to the world's battlefields, helping the wounded soldiers of all armies. Different names were bandied about for what to call it, and meanwhile, Dunant got to work on its symbol. He wanted it to be unmistakably neutral, and distinctive also to the combatants. It had to be recognisable from long distance, so the doctors would not be shelled by mistake. The flag of Switzerland, already known as a neutral country, was the obvious choice, except to the Swiss authorities. So instead, the Swiss flag was reversed, and the new aid organisation was named for its symbol. In 1863 the Red Cross was born.

Dunant was lauded for the achievement, but he wanted more. He began lobbying other nations to sign a convention promising to protect the wounded on the battlefield. The lobbying effort was hard, but Dunant was energetic. He criss-crossed Europe to meet governments and urge support at conferences. During the lobbying process, he continually changed his proposed convention. One night in Berlin, he and a friend sat up late into the night rewriting it for a conference speech the next day. The following morning they took an open carriage across the city. As they crossed the River Spree, a wind whipped across the bridge, blowing the one and only copy of their convention into the water. Dunant, his friend and a bystander scrambled into the river to retrieve the pages.

Rules of war were as old as war itself. Europe had its chivalry rules, Japan the Samurai code. But those codes were aimed more at protecting important combatants. At Agincourt in 1415, both sides took care to capture rather than kill fallen knights, but were happy to execute common soldiers. What was new about Dunant's code was that it was humanitarian, applying to all wounded troops.

The lobbying worked, and in August 1864 the Swiss government hosted a formal conference where twelve states signed it. For want of a better name, the agreement was named after the city where it was signed, and the first Geneva Convention was born.

That first convention is only a page long. The reason it took Dunant so many drafts was not because of what was in it, but what was left out. Governments were unwilling to sign off on further measures, like caring for prisoners and civilians, although those were inserted into subsequent, expanded Geneva Conventions. That first convention shaped the war laws that followed. Largely because war law is simple. It is designed to be that way, so armies in the field can understand it. Like other war laws, it takes the form of a list. In Geneva's case, a list of guarantees for non-combatants on the battlefield.

Geneva established something else too, a crude bargain between humanitarians and warriors. Humanitarians realised early on that battlefields could not be policed, because the most powerful forces were the armies themselves. So instead, they appealed to the generals to do no harm that was not necessary to win. It was crude, and difficult to measure, but it was a bargain that governments were willing to go along with.

Geneva law is one of the two key pieces of modern war law. What would become the other half had been issued a year earlier, on the other side of the Atlantic.

That law started life as the US Army's General Orders 100, later to be adopted as the Hague Convention. It has many of the same obligations as Geneva law, but pitched from a different direction. Instead of listing the protected groups, Hague law is a set of dos and don'ts for armies. The wounded and prisoners are to be cared for, civilians are not to be attacked.

General Orders 100 was created by another maverick, Franz Lieber, originally from Prussia. Like Dunant, Lieber was scarred by war. In his case, he had been wounded as a young Prussian soldier at Waterloo. Before settling on the law, he'd tried mathematics, topography, poetry, education, gymnastics and encyclopaedia editing. He left Prussia after being twice jailed for agitating against the government, and fought as a volunteer in the Greek war of independence. He arrived in the United States to teach gymnastics but switched to the law. By the time the civil war broke out in 1861 he was working as a professor at New York's Columbia University.

Abraham Lincoln chose him to write the new army code, reasoning that, as a non-American, Lieber was more likely to be seen as a neutral by both sides. The impetus for the new law was very different to the Geneva Convention. It came from Union generals, who found the Confederate forces they were fighting were often armed civilians rather than enlisted troops. They wanted legal protection against being charged with murder for killing such civilians. The new law, paradoxically, was written to keep generals out of jail rather than clean up the battlefield.

And the new law also grasped the thorny issue sidestepped with the Geneva Convention. Geneva law was built on the assumption that attacks on non-combatants had no military purpose, and so could be outlawed. Lieber recognised that sometimes attacks on civilians did serve a military purpose. At least, from the general's point of view. And so, into his code, Lieber inserted a qualification. The long list of dos and don'ts could be ignored in the case of 'military necessity'. The year after his code became law, Union generals took him at his word. By 1864 the civil war had developed into a slug-fest. Union armies were more powerful than the Confederates, but the frontlines stretched more than a thousand miles. That made it difficult to pin down Confederate forces. So, instead, the Union decided to target the population those forces depended on.

The first of two huge campaigns was launched in the east. Cavalry general Philip Sheridan led Union forces down the long, broad Shenandoah Valley, destroying everything in his path. Farms and villages were burned, crops destroyed, livestock either taken or slaughtered. Soon, tens of thousands of civilians were left destitute. The Confederate forces remained elusive, but now they had lost their food supply. Many soldiers deserted to help their families survive.

A still greater offensive was then mounted in Georgia by General William Sherman. The objective was simply to smash the South's economy. He began by burning Atlanta, the state capital. Then the army set off on a march east to the sea, scything a thirty-mile-wide corridor of destruction through the state. Towns were laid waste, factories burned and railroads torn up. 'Sherman's March' has remained controversial ever since, but from a military point of view it worked. The Confederacy's war-making powers were smashed. Surrender came six months later, by which time the army of Robert E. Lee was half-starved. Total war delivered Lincoln victory, and left the South devastated. Sympathy was in short supply in the Union, which remembered the millions of brutalised slaves that had powered the Confederate economy. For critics, the main effect of General Orders Number 100 was to keep Union generals out of prison, rather than jail war criminals. Nevertheless, Lieber's code lays claim to being the first modern codification of war law. It was enshrined in the Hague Conventions of 1899 and 1907, becoming one of the bedrocks of war law.

Neither the Hague nor the Geneva Convention is a work of genius. Looking down their respective lists, most of what they state is obvious. You could write it yourself. What was unusual was not the rules, but the fact that governments on both sides of the Atlantic signed on to them, inside a single year. One big reason was the advent of industrial war, and the shock of how deadly war had become. What sep-arated Waterloo from the clashes at Solferino and the US civil war was the industrial revolution. The technological upheaval powered by steam led to a quantum leap in what armies could do to each other.

In a few decades, weapons had become more deadly. The inaccurate smooth-bore slow-loading muskets of Waterloo were giving way to fast-firing rifled weapons with vastly improved accuracy. Cannon balls had given way to shells filled with high explosive. The new factories meant those weapons could be turned out in huge quantities, and the new railways meant they could be transported fast to the front. Napoleon's army at Solferino was the first in history to arrive for the campaign by rail. Yet while weapons were more lethal, soldiers had no better protection than before. Armies still went into battle on horseback or at marching pace, and the butcher's bill skyrocketed. The US civil war cost over 600,000 deaths, equivalent to the toll of all America's other wars put together.

What galvanised politicians on both sides of the Atlantic was that still deadlier weapons were on the horizon. Richard Jordan Gatling had already produced the first machine gun and German chemists were experimenting with poison gas. At sea, steam-powered ironclads were replacing wooden sailing ships.

A still greater shock propelled the creation of the third arm of modern war law, designed to deal with the worst crime of all. Its architect was Raphael Lemkin, a Polish-Jewish lawyer raised in a farm near the town of Bialystok in what was then Russian-occupied Poland.

Lemkin was born in 1900, the year before Dunant won the first ever Nobel Peace Prize. Like Dunant and Lieber, he had personal experience of slaughter, having grown up in the shadow of anti-Jewish pogroms all over Poland. He was five years old when at least eighty Jews were killed, and many more injured, by Moscow-backed mobs rampaging through Jewish homes and businesses in Bialystok. When he was fourteen, the First World War broke out and German forces occupied his part of Poland. His farm was burned and his family fled to the forest, where one of his brothers died from pneumonia. At the end of the occupation, once Poland had gained independence, he studied law, developing a fixation with pogroms. His preoccupation was with why people could be massacred not for anything they had done, but simply for who they were.

Lemkin quickly emerged as a skilful lawyer, and opted to campaign for human rights. He represented Poland at several international conferences, making contacts who would later save his life. In 1939 Germany's Blitzkrieg ripped into Poland and Lemkin was able to flee to Sweden, thanks to a contact who got him a visa. Another contact secured him an official invitation to the United States, which he reached via a rail journey across the USSR shortly before it was invaded by Germany. His family were not so lucky, forty-nine of them perishing in the Holocaust.

In America, Lemkin lectured at Duke University in North Carolina and wrote a book charting Hitler's occupation of Europe. But he wanted more. He had already researched a history of pogroms, stretching from ancient times and including Turkey's massacre of Armenians in the 1920s. There was no name to describe such crimes, so Lemkin invented one. He combined the Ancient Greek word for people, *genos*, with the Latin suffix for killing, *caedere*, and coined the word 'genocide'.

What followed was a Dunant-style campaign to create a genocide convention. Lemkin badgered and agitated everyone he could think of to win support. Aiding him was the shock that came at the end of the war with the discovery of the full horror of Hitler's concentration camps. The fact that Germany had created what amounted to factories to destroy human life appalled people in the victorious states. It set the seal on a war judged uniquely horrific, sitting alongside the slaughter of twenty million Russians, and Japan's mass starvation of its occupied territories and experimentation programmes on live victims. Impelled by the hope of avoiding a repeat, a new organisation called the United Nations was formed in October 1945, the impetus being to stop future wars. It had a general assembly to give every nation a voice, and a top table, the Security Council. The council was created to be a sort of permanent peace conference, able to deal with crises as they came up. One of the first decisions by the UN's general assembly, made up of all the states in the world, was to agree a Genocide Convention, passed in 1948.

More treaties and conventions followed, widening war law to cover mass crimes perpetuated outside of formal states of war. By 1948 the big three arms of war law were in place. More conventions followed, dealing with torture and chemical weapons, as did the UN's Universal Declaration of Human Rights. What was missing – and this was where governments put their foot down – was a way of enforcing them.

The Nuremberg and Tokyo war crimes trials, held after the war, were arguably the first proper war crimes trials. The evidence was strong, the procedure sturdy, but it was victor's justice. Carpet bombing of civilians was judged, but not when carried out by allied powers. A general war crimes court had little support from the UN.

Instead, the UN created the International Court of Justice. Its home is the Peace Palace, a gothic masterpiece in The Hague. The palace itself is a historic quirk, created not by governments but by American industrialist Andrew Carnegie, who was galvanised by the Hague Conventions. With war clouds massing over Europe, he wanted to have some way of enforcing the new rules. So he paid $1.5 million to create the world's first war crimes court. Public support was high, and donations flooded in from around the world. The palace features marble from Italy, chandeliers from Austria, silk tapestries from Japan and rugs from Persia. Britain donated the stained-glass windows and Russia's Tsar gifted a three-tonne vase.

Having commissioned the palace, Carnegie dared the world powers to ignore the public desire to set up a war crimes court. His pressure worked, to the extent that the world's governments created the Permanent Court of Arbitration to sit in the new palace. That court had yet to hear a case when the First World War broke out.

When the war was over, a League of Nations was set up, in an early attempt to create a world-wide organisation to maintain peace. Its legal arm, the Permanent Court of International Justice, was housed in the

Peace Palace. After the League, and its court, were swept away by the Second World War, the world tried collective security again with the formation of the UN. Its court, the International Court of Justice, became the third tenant to be installed at the Peace Palace.

The reason you have likely not heard of the ICJ is that the UN powers were united in determination to clip its wings. The ICJ was not empowered to enforce The Hague, Geneva or Genocide Conventions. Instead, it is limited to arbitrating disputes between states. ICJ judges can penalise states, but not individuals, and impose fines, but no jail terms. The final kicker is that the court can only take a case if both sides agree to it being heard. Unsurprisingly, many powers guilty of war crimes choose not to let the ICJ hear their dispute.

Where the ICJ does occasionally make headlines is through advisory opinions. In 2003 it ruled against the border wall constructed by Israel along part of its eastern border with the Palestinian West Bank. The judgment did not rule the wall itself illegal, only the parts positioned in occupied Palestinian territory. In theory Israel could move the wall behind its own borders and escape censure.

The ruling was requested by the UN general assembly, but with Israel refusing to be party to any arbitration, the ruling remains advisory. Advisory, and obvious. It made no comment on the building of walls, only on where they were built.

The Cold War dominated the first decades of the UN, stifling any attempts to find a way to make war crimes conventions enforceable. Instead, the idea remained fanciful. The Cold War world saw nations scramble to sign dozens more conventions, safe in the knowledge there would never be courts to try them. To reinforce that fact, it turned out there was a big difference between a state agreeing a convention and ratifying it – that is, incorporating it into the state's own law. The Genocide Convention, proclaimed with strident speeches in 1948, took three years to gain just twenty ratifications. The USA, the country of its birth, only ratified it in 1988. This had a profound effect on Lemkin, who judged his work a failure. Sure, world leaders were happy to announce that genocide was wrong, but that was as far as it went. Like Lieber, Lemkin died in New York City. But unlike Lieber, he died a broken man. Only a handful of people attended his funeral. Near the end, he told one of his few friends, 'The fact is that the rain of my work fell on a fallow plain.'

〉 〉 〉 ▶ ▶ ▶

The key to understanding international war crimes courts is to realise they were created almost by accident. There never was a plan by the UN or anyone else to set them up; their existence is down to a freak historical occurrence.

In 1992, Serb forces rampaged through Bosnia, one region of the former state of Yugoslavia. Their target was its Croat and Muslim population. That rampage killed 100,000, caused three million to flee, besieged Sarajevo and saw the return to Europe of concentration camps. Serb commanders introduced a new phrase into the world's lexicon: ethnic cleansing.

World powers were stumped. They were still in the post-coital glow from the end of the Cold War when the collapse of the Soviet Union had seemed to usher in a new era of peace. Democracy was breaking out across the globe. American president George H. W. Bush had proclaimed a 'New World Order'. American political scientist Francis Fukuyama caught the global mood with his book *The End of History and the Last Man*. In it, he proclaimed that after centuries of strife, the world had arrived at the end point of historical development, which was liberal democracy. All other forms of government, he declared, had proven to have failed. Serb ethnic cleansing broke out the same year Fukuyama's book was published, and the shockwaves were felt across the world's growing democracies.

Yet those democracies did not want to intervene in Bosnia. Nato had massive armies left over from the Cold War, but hesitated to deploy them for peace-keeping. Politicians worried that the political support for intervention would dry up when the first body bags came home. So, to buy off public opinion, they determined to do everything short of intervention.

In April 1993 a young American lawyer named Larry Johnson found out what that meant. Johnson was a gregarious and optimistic Harvard law graduate who had opted to work for the UN in inter-national law. That day, he was in Iowa City, having volunteered to explain to students there the workings of international law. Arriving back at his hotel that night, he found a message to call UN headquarters. He got on the phone to find out that the world powers had decided to set up a war crimes court for Bosnia. And that he was one of a six-strong team designated to write the rules.

The court was the brainchild of America's UN ambassador, Madeleine Albright. Like Dunant and Lieber and Lemkin, she had direct experience of the horrors of war. As a child, her family had fled not once but twice from her native Czechoslovakia, first from Hitler's invasion and later from Stalin's communism. In between, she had endured Hitler's Blitz in London, and had even been interviewed, shuddering under the bombs, by a film crew there. Albright was central in providing the impetus for the UN to set up a war crimes court, but some questioned America's motives, saying Washington was putting its energy into setting up the court in order to deflect attention from its refusal to provide UN peacekeepers for Bosnia. 'Cynics in the [UN General] Assembly said this was a Madeleine Albright initiative to defend European criticism of the US for not putting troops on the ground in Bosnia,' said Johnson later.

Governments of all stripes are reluctant to support war crimes courts. Not because they are especially callous, but because they dislike creating legal mechanisms that are beyond their ability to control. The new war crimes court had full powers, but those powers were limited to Bosnia and the states of former Yugoslavia. The rest of the world was not included. Such influence as the new court acquired was in part the result of activists, some of them state officials, pushing reluctant politicians into making good on promises to support justice. James O'Brien, a State Department lawyer who provided key evidence to bolster American support for that first court, explained how it worked. The US government would declare that it supported a war crimes court in principle. So O'Brien and others would provide the evidence that a court could be made to work, almost daring the politicians to reject it: 'The way it worked was that by pushing this and showing it was possible, people were in a position where they had to say no. And nobody wants to say no to justice.'

Johnson's team worked the same way. They decided among themselves that the war crimes court had only moderate support at the UN. If the rules they were drafted were vague, many states would have the excuse to declare the court was a good idea, but not practical. So they worked hard to make sure the rules were sturdy. Those rules are the template for the International Criminal Court that came later. The Hague, Geneva and Genocide Conventions were included, along with a mass of other treaties. One clause – designed to conform with one of the bedrock principles of law, which is that you cannot be tried for breaking a law that did not exist at the time you broke it – was that anything could be included if the former Yugoslavia had already signed up to it. Luckily for Johnson, Yugoslavia had joined other states in signing a mass of human rights conventions after the Second World War.

That six-strong team also shaped modern war law. Its provisions are divided into three parts. War crimes fleshes out the Hague Convention, dealing with battlefield crimes. Crimes against humanity covers atrocities when the war itself is directed at civilians. And genocide is for the crime-of-crimes; in legal terms, it covers the same ground as crimes against humanity, except that it applies when the horrors are aimed at a specific group.

Johnson was imbued with the same triumph as earlier war law pioneers when the rules for the new court were approved by the UN. 'It felt like a Frankenstein movie,' he said. 'You make this creature by borrowing bits and pieces of different things, a bit from the Geneva Conventions, something from Hague law, other bits from other places. And instead of a bolt of lightning, this thing gets a Chapter Seven energy infusion from the Security Council. Then you bring it back down, and damn it, it's alive.'

That first UN court, the clunkily named International Criminal Tribunal for the former Yugoslavia (ICTY), endured the same difficulties as the ICC does today: war crimes courts may be international, but they depend on national governments both for money, and for police forces to bring in the suspects. Neither was forthcoming for the ICTY. Its first president, Antonio Cassese, had so little money that he began work with a staff of four. There was no money for a courthouse, so instead the tribunal operated out of borrowed rooms at the Peace Palace. To save money, Cassese did without a company car and rode to work by bike. The first chief prosecutor was South Africa's Richard Goldstone, famous for spearheading a commission named after him to help bring peace in the post-Apartheid era. When he flew to New York to accept the job from the UN, he was obliged to pay for his own air ticket. He was later allowed to claim it back on expenses, but it set the tone for the lack of political support for the tribunal. The Bosnian war ended in 1995 with the cash-starved court yet to hold a single trial. It might have stayed that way, except for a chance intervention by Madeleine Albright.

She visited the court at the Peace Palace and was shocked at the cash-strapped reality. Back in America, she assembled a team of twenty-two lawyers and FBI investigators and dispatched them to The Hague, paid for by the US government. With them went law books and even tables and chairs. Her action probably saved the court.

Her action by itself didn't make war crimes courts a success, but it meant they had become too big to die. That one court also created a cascade effect. In 1994 a still greater genocide broke out in Rwanda. Ethnic Hutu extremists killed more than 800,000 Tutsis and moderate Hutus in the greatest slaughter since the Second World War. Having created a war crimes court for Bosnia, the UN felt obliged to create a second one for Rwanda. To save money, they insisted that the courts share a prosecutor, with the result that Goldstone had to spend much of his time commuting between two courthouses on separate continents. Nevertheless, having agreed those courts, the UN felt similarly obliged to deal with fresh wars in Cambodia, East Timor and Sierra Leone by setting up still more temporary courts.

That, in turn, created the momentum for the International Criminal Court. Logic dictated that instead of the UN setting up a new court each time a war broke out, it should establish a permanent tribunal. One comparison was with the idea of a small town dealing with fires by creating a fire engine for each fresh blaze. Simpler, surely, to just have a fire engine on permanent standby. Such progress sounds seamless, yet it was anything but. Creating war crimes courts was one thing, making them effective was something else. And on that, the great powers were unenthusiastic. Madeleine Albright may have jump-started the first UN court, but her involvement was a one-off. America's Clinton administration was thereafter as lukewarm as other governments about supporting the tribunal's work. That reluctance was felt in one key area: the lack of arrests. The tribunal had no police force of its own, and no way of making suspects come to court. Only outside powers could do that. Goldstone described those powers as the 'arms and legs' of the court. Without them, he was powerless.

Yet for every crisis, the tribunals seemed to have a limitless reserve of lawyers with the drive and political calculation to get what was needed. Goldstone's replacement was Canadian judge Louise Arbour, a diminutive and motivated woman who staffers said could be both ruthless and charming. When the Bosnian war ended, with not a single war crimes trial having been held, the big powers were happy to forget about the court. Fifty thousand Nato-led peacekeepers were deployed to Bosnia, but their political overlords told them not to go after the war crimes suspects being busily indicted by The Hague. Arbour made her little chunk of history one day in 1996 when she was invited to give a short fifteen-minute presentation at a meeting of the Nato powers. She decided on a bold approach. Instead of asking that Nato troops be used to catch her suspects, she demanded it. She told the surprised delegates that the duty to arrest suspects was in fact a little-visited part of the Bosnian peace plan. Years later, she told me: 'I told them this is not a matter of political choice, it is the law and you have to do it.'

Arbour sat back down to stunned silence, but her demand worked. A few months later, American, British, French and Dutch special forces began raids, bringing in more than thirty suspects.

⟩ ⟩ ⟩ ⟩ ⟩ ⟩

Arbour got the headlines, but it was a feature of the early war crimes courts that they drew on the ideal-istic sentiments of their lawyers. It became common for leading criminal lawyers to volunteer for stretches at the tribunals: to help justice, according to their fans; to win fame, according to their critics. The suc-cess of the UN courts was to show that war law, fine in theory, was also fine in practice. It turned out that abstract laws could be turned into operable criminal law. For this reason, the great powers were happy to let the tribunals continue. Where many drew the line was at the suggestion that war crimes justice be made universal.

By the latter 1990s the UN had started work on establishing the International Criminal Court to replace its temporary courts. It was then obliged to stop after objections from China, Russia and the United States. Those powers matter because they are among the permanent five members (P5) of the UN Security Council, the most powerful body on earth. What makes the P5, which also includes Britain and France, so strong is that they have a veto on anything of importance the UN does. Including the creation of war crimes courts.

With three of the P5 objecting to a world court, the idea was dropped. And then picked up again by the powers in favour. The ICC came into being in July 2002, although less as a worldwide tribunal than a private members' club. The ICC 'club' is run by its member states, and has jurisdiction over them. From the start, it was hamstrung by its most obvious limitation – states that commit war crimes don't join international war crimes courts.

The ICC rules are built to try and extend its reach. They give the UN Security Council the power to order it to investigate war crimes in non-member states. This has been done twice, in Libya and Sudan, although ICC staffers complained that the UN did not advance them much extra money to cover the investigations. The ICC also allows non-member states to ask it to investigate crimes on their territory, as has happened with Ukraine. In practice any state can do it. One ICC staffer told me how, when the American-led Iraq invasion began in 2003, a small team clustered around the fax machine in the prosecutor's office. They were waiting to see if Saddam Hussein would fax a formal request for the ICC to have jurisdiction over Iraq. It was as simple as that: one fax would have done it. But no fax arrived, and the governments who replaced Hussein have never requested ICC coverage.

The ICC followed the guidelines Johnson's team had set out for the first UN courts, establishing the same three kinds of crime: war crimes, for crimes on the battlefield; crimes against humanity, for when the civilian population is the target of the war; and genocide. Among those first ICC staffers, the reality that much of the world remained out of its reach did not dampen their enthusiasm for the cause. They reasoned that, while the ICC was not a world court, it could still aim to become one. The dream went like this: With the advent of the ICC, the world would divide in two. On one side, that part of the world subject to the rule of law. On the other, the part where the people with the guns made the rules. Over time, they felt, the peace and prosperity of states operating under the law would become obvious to all. More and more nations would clamour to join the ICC. The ICC might only deal with war crimes, but membership would act as a roof under which the rule of law could put down roots.

That dream was on show one day in 2003 when the worlds of law and power collided in a single building.

The building was the sleek slab of steel and glass that is the UN headquarters on New York's East River. The date was 5 February. Downstairs, the newly created ICC was choosing its first group of judges. Upstairs, America's secretary of state Colin Powell was making his infamous case for invading Iraq.

Powell had a difficult task in explaining why America and its British ally were about to launch their attack, because it broke the UN Charter. The Charter allows war in only two circumstances: either to defend from attack, or because it is authorised by the UN Security Council. Authorisation by the Council was out, with France, China and Russia all indicating they would vote against it. For that reason, America and Britain decided not to ask. Instead, Powell said, the war was defensive, because Saddam Hussein was ready to attack with biological, chemical and nuclear weapons, the so-called weapons of mass destruction (WMD). Most of Powell's speech was spent detailing evidence, later proved to have been fabricated, of Iraq's massive stocks of WMD.

'My colleagues, every statement I make today is backed up by sources, solid sources,' he announced. 'These are not assertions. What we're giving you are facts and conclusions based on solid intelligence.'

Downstairs, the meeting to select the first judges for the ICC was underway. Delegates paused to watch Powell's speech on the TV monitors. None yet knew that the evidence was a lie, and that Iraq had no WMD. What they did know was that London and Washington were preparing to launch an illegal war. Illegal but, because there was no criminal court to enforce the UN Charter, unpreventable. Britain and America were going to war not because it was legal, but because they could. It was a vivid demonstration of might-is-right.

Symbolism lay heavy in the building that day. Shortly before Powell gave his speech, officials covered up a tapestry that hangs in the Security Council lobby. It is a black-and-white reproduction of Picasso's painting *Guernica*, an iconic protest against the horrors of war. Powell was due to take questions from the media there, and US officials did not want him talking with that image as the backdrop. So, for one time only, a blue curtain was draped over the painting.

Another symbol was the upstairs-downstairs nature of the two meetings. The power of might-is-right was on full display in the Security Council, while the alternative world view of rule-of-law was confined to the basement. America and Britain were preparing to spend billions on their new war. By contrast the ICC was having to count the pennies. Budgetary problems were the reason the ICC, based in The Hague, was holding its meeting on the far side of the Atlantic. The UN headquarters was the one place in the world where all ICC member states already had diplomatic delegations. There was no need to pay to fly people in and find them hotels. The voting could be done by diplomats already in place.

The UN made sure to underline that the court was nothing to do with them, by obliging the ICC to pay for the week-long hire of the UN basement conference hall. UN press officers were at pains to emphasise that although the new court was hiring its hall, the two organisations were separate. That distinction was missed by many, including the *New York Times*. Its report of the ICC judge-selection process was headlined 'UN Court'.

Down in the basement, ICC officials knew it would be months before the new court was ready for action, and years before it could hold its first trials. But most were optimistic. In their mind, the old world, where the powerful did what they liked, would surely now be superseded by the new, where the law was supreme. The dream of enforcing war law, extending back to that first Geneva Convention, was finally a reality. 'The train has left the station,' one excited Dutch delegate told me at the end. As it turned out, he was wrong.

In the twenty years that followed, the ICC managed just one conviction every four years. Those five convictions are strong cases: three were warlords from the Democratic Republic of Congo, and one from Uganda. The fifth, Ahmad al-Mahdi, was jailed for destroying historic and religious monuments in Timbuktu. There were another five convictions for witness tampering, bringing the total conviction record to ten. Yet this compares poorly to what the UN courts achieved: the ICTY operated for twenty-five years and jailed ninety war criminals. The UN's Rwanda tribunal jailed sixty-one.

Blue Sky Duds

There is no shortage of blue sky thinking on how to make the ICC, and war crimes law in general, more effective. Law school conferences and human rights groups teem with ideas and theories.

The most obvious way to extend war crimes justice across the world is for the nations controlling the ICC to declare it a universal court. At their annual conference, the Assembly of States Parties, they could change the constitution to give their court a worldwide brief.

That will not happen, because the states inside the ICC fear the reaction from the states outside. Those include not just the key powers of China, Russia and the United States, but a galaxy of regional players. Among them are Egypt, India, Iraq, Iran, Israel,

Pakistan, Saudi Arabia and North Korea. None are likely to countenance the ICC being able to simply declare jurisdiction over their affairs. For the same reason, the United Nations cannot adopt the ICC as its own court, as those nations, and many others, would object.

With the ICC likely to remain limited as to which states it can cover, thoughts have turned to alternative war crimes courts. The UN had success with its five war crimes courts set up in the 1990s. Maybe, some wonder, that might be the model for the future. When a war breaks out in the world, a war crimes court will be set up to deal with it. The problem is that Russia's invasion of Ukraine has in effect broken the Security Council. Of the five permanent members, Moscow has launched a war in direct defiance of the UN Charter, while the USA, Britain and France are arming Ukraine. Russia was never enthusiastic about war crimes courts, but in the past went along with UN plans to create them. That changed when the ICC indicted Putin. Russia's current leadership is now hostile to the idea of war crimes courts, and will almost certainly use its veto to block the creation of new ones by the Security Council. Collective action on setting up new war crimes courts is extremely unlikely in this atmosphere.

Alternatively, new courts can be set up by like-minded nations. More thirty states have already indicated outline support for a special tribunal to investigate Russia for the crime of aggression in Ukraine.

The crime of aggression is different to other war law in that it targets the war itself, rather than offences committed in that war. It was the centrepiece of the Nuremberg and Tokyo tribunals after the Second World War. Since then, it has faded from view. It was not included in the remit of the UN temporary war crimes courts. The crime became the fourth dealt with by the ICC in 2010, but there were restrictions. These state that the court can only prosecute ICC members who commit aggression, not non-members who invade them.

That is another difference from the other crimes on the statute. Anybody can be indicted for those, provided only that the crime is committed on ICC territory. The compromise was made because ICC member states did not want to antagonise allies who were non-members. In support of the new tribunal, in early 2023 the European Union set up a fact-finding office in The Hague to gather material for the proposed court. No final decision had been made on setting it up at the time of publication, but the idea has serious drawbacks.

First, the new tribunal is no more likely to arrest
Russian suspects than the ICC. That would leave it
looking like an expensive failure as the years pass
with the jail and dock empty. And it would not
be the first. In 2009, the United Nations set up a
Special Tribunal for Lebanon, also to investigate
just one crime: the suicide car-bombing that killed
former Lebanese prime minister Rafic Hariri and
twenty-one others in Beirut in 2005. Originally it
was due to run for three years and cost $120 million.
In the end, it ran for eleven years, cost $450 million
and jailed nobody. Three suspects were found guilty
in their absence, a quirk of the court allowing trials
in absentia. All were given life sentences, but none
can be found. Nor did the court get to the bottom of
who planned the assassination. Judges closed the case
declaring that while the three convicts had planned
it, there was no evidence of any wider organisation
or state being involved. In war law legend, it is des-
tined to go down as the court that never held a trial.

The crime of aggression tribunal will also face
a credibility problem if it is limited only to Russia.
Critics have noted that one of the tribunal's key backers is former British prime minister Gordon Brown.
He was a member of a Labour government that twice
launched wars which, under this tribunal's rules,

would be considered crimes of aggression: intervention in Kosovo in 1999 and the Iraq invasion four years later. Neither operation was defensive, and neither was backed by the UN Security Council, the only two kinds of wars acceptable under the UN Charter. The thirty states supporting it are saying, in effect, that it will try Russia for a crime that does not apply to them.

Many have pointed out that if there is to be a crime of aggression tribunal, it would be quicker, and cheaper, for the ICC to do the job. The ICC's first prosecutor, Luis Moreno Ocampo, pointed out in a letter that the ICC could do so simply by changing one paragraph of its rules: that limiting the crime to ICC members only.

The fact that most ICC member states won't change that paragraph highlights the lack of credibility the new court would have. If most of the world's states object to the new court, its authority is limited. It would be easier for the states supporting the court to save the hundreds of millions of dollars it will cost and simply declare Putin and the Kremlin guilty of the offence.

That is not to say the special court for the crime of aggression will not happen, only that it will not work.

Other initiatives to broaden the reach of war crimes justice include putting the sanctions aimed at Russia on a legal footing. Why not, some ask, have international laws mandating sanctions on any state committing war crimes? The answer is because states want to keep sanctions powers for themselves, not hand them to a legal body. For all these possible initiatives, the same obstacle remains. Which is that only governments can set up war crimes courts, and most are reluctant to do so.

So if courts cannot stop war crimes across the world, what can? South Africa pioneered the use of truth and reconciliation commissions to bring closure, if not justice. These commissions operate under a simple premise. Anyone who committed crimes can be forgiven, provided they make a detailed confession. The commissions were lauded as a successful means of bringing down the curtain on the Apartheid era. Some countries have copied the model, notably Sierra Leone.

The problem with truth and reconciliation commissions is that they do not deter war crimes. Not when a warlord knows they can commit murder and mayhem, then escape punishment just by admitting what they did. As a one-off system, confessional forgiveness can bring dividends. As a means of ending the world's war crimes, it is a dud.

War crimes courts are not an end to themselves, but a tool. They exist in order to punish the worst offences on the planet, but also to deter them from happening in the first place. That has led some researchers to look at who commits war crimes, and whether they can be stopped.

>))) ▶ ▶ ▶

The first detailed psychological research into atrocities and who commits them was done in the United States during the Vietnam War. The motivation was the My Lai massacre in 1968. One bright morning, a company of the 28th Infantry Division arrived at a group of hamlets set by the sea, and began killing. When the day was over, at least 350 men, women and children were slaughtered.

The shocking massacre prompted a wave of studies into atrocities and who commits them. Psychiatrists across America started reporting a surge of ex-soldiers confessing to crimes. Putting the data together, they realised they could profile those most likely to commit atrocities.

Statistically, they were more likely to be from a rural than a city background. More likely to be nineteen or under. At school, more likely to prefer team games, with a defined opponent, than solo sports like athletics. More likely, also, to have had a troubled home life. One surprising finding was that atrocities were not generally committed by the loud, aggressive members of a unit, but the quiet ones. Intelligence was not a factor as perpetrators were as likely to have a high IQ as a low one. But they tended to be men who struggled with personal relationships. Men who related better to 'things' than people. Awkwardly for the army, they also tended to be more successful soldiers.

It was more likely that they had volunteered for the army than been conscripted. More likely that, once in action, they gravitated to higher-stressed posts, like radio operator and point-man. They were three times as likely to have won a medal, twice as likely to have been wounded.

The Pentagon got serious about studying the problem. And that study had a dark side. A British journalist with the *Sunday Times*, Peter Watson, dug out evidence of mind-control experiments being conducted at the US Naval Neuropsychiatric Research Centre in San Diego. He was refused access, but sources told him scientists were trying not to dampen enthusiasm for atrocities but encourage it. Or anyway, to inure personnel to the horrors of war. There were *Clockwork Orange*-style experiments, with recruits having their heads put in vices, then forced to watch hours of gruesome films. The hope was that it would remove inhibitions. Why the navy, rather than the army, took the lead he was unable to explain. In his book *War on the Mind* Watson traces all kinds of mind control experiments among armies the world over: brainwashing, interrogation techniques and more. Decades on, there is no sign yet of conscience-free 'super soldiers' taking to the battlefield. Depressingly, that is partly because they are not needed. There are enough recruits willing to do the barely imaginable anyway. Armies have structures and discipline to keep a lid on it, but militias have none.

More depressing was maybe the most controversial psychological study ever attempted: the Stanford Prison Experiment.

In 1971, a US Navy-funded Stanford University professor, Philip Zimbardo, tricked out the basement of the university's psychology department as a makeshift jail. Then he filled it with volunteers. The volunteers were students and were randomly divided into two groups: guards and inmates. The inmates had their heads shaved, the guards were given khaki uniforms and mirror shades. Then they were told to get on with it.

Zimbardo had stipulated that there could be no violence, which was probably a good thing. Because within a few days the guards had developed a sadistic regime for the prisoners. In turn, the inmates meekly complied. Soon screams and shouts echoed down the corridors. The experiment was set to last for a fortnight, but university authorities, shocked by what they saw, terminated it after six days.

Disputes have raged ever since about the validity of this chaos as an authentic experiment. For Zimbardo, they were a real-life version of William Golding's novel *Lord of the Flies*, where a group of schoolboys turns feral when left unsupervised on a desert island. Zimbardo's view was that we all have a switch in our heads. In the right circumstances, that switch can be flipped.

That study shows how 'normal' people can turn savage, but doesn't explain the existence of militias where volunteers join specifically to be brutal.

German researchers from the University of Konstanz studied veterans of the Hutu militias responsible for the Rwandan genocide. Later, a Tutsi-led army gained control and the paramilitaries fled into neighbouring Congo. Here, the researchers spent months interviewing them. Their first surprise was that the militiamen were happy to confess their crimes. The second was that they had enjoyed it. Many told them that killing gave them a thrill they had not known in civilian life. One talked of feeling a 'thirst' for his favoured operations, which were attacks on villages. He would kill the men, rape whatever women he found, and burn the houses.

British investigators had found similar yearnings among Nazi extremists captured in the Second World War. A group of eight notorious SS men were studied in detail. All had committed atrocities. All had similar backgrounds: all had been raised in rural communities, in modest homes, had experienced trouble with their parents and had achieved low school grades. They had made no mark on the world until they joined the SS.

The British studies also found a big difference between the leaders and the led. One leader studied in depth was Kurt Meyer, commander of the 12 SS Panzer division. The division was formed from teenage members of the Hitler Youth, in the belief they would kill without conscience. Meyer was captured in 1944. Absurdly, for a self-proclaimed warrior, he surrendered to a Belgian farmer who found him cowering in a barn. Shipped to Britain, he was put in a hut with other Nazi chiefs in a prison camp, Trent Park. Then the hut was bugged.

In private, Meyer acted the part of the strutting Nazi. He proclaimed his love of Hitler, and berated comrades who expressed doubts. But researchers became aware that there was something else going on. They came to believe that Nazism had not turned Meyer into a fanatic. Instead, the fanaticism had come first. Nazism was for him the outlet. They came to think there is such a thing as the born fanatic.

This seemed to be confirmed by the priority he gave to self-preservation. A true believer would have gone down in a blaze of glory, rather than cower in a hayloft. Meyer committed war crimes in Poland, Russia and France, but was tried for only one case: the murder of Canadian prisoners of war in Normandy. He was sentenced to death, at which point his ideological beliefs faded and he begged for mercy. His luck was that his appeal was heard by a Canadian general who had also committed what would today be a war crime: he ordered an abandoned village burned to the ground in revenge for the death of a fellow officer.

In prison, Meyer dropped his fanaticism and became a model prisoner. Back in the world, he was a model citizen, staying out of trouble. In the end, the allies let him run an association for German former SS men. This was likely because it was believed Meyer's ultimate loyalty was to himself. As leader, he could persuade the more wayward members not to return to violence.

Meyer's history fits with a great truth about defeated militias. When the hammer comes down, the leaders simply revert to normal life, untroubled by conscience. By contrast, their foot soldiers are left bewildered, angry, and sometimes troubled by the horrors they have inflicted.

Militias, indeed all extremist groups, act like a debt consolidation service. Join a militia, and all the frustrations and compromises of civilian life are forgotten. Now, all those problems are rolling into one big problem, and that problem is *them*. The enemy might be a state or a group or nationality. Whatever it is, they are all that stands between you and happiness. Destroy *them*, and your problems go away.

Psychology Today writer Peter Doskoch described militiamen he interviewed as craving acceptance. Militias, he said, attract people who can't fit in anywhere else. The militias in question were not in a war zone, but in the rural United States.

❯ ❯ ❯ ❯ ❯ ❯

Armed forces across the world devote attention to educating troops about war crimes, and to finding operating procedures that will avoid them. That includes ensuring firm command and control, in order to avoid the chaos that produced the My Lai massacre. Preparing soldiers for the din of battle, and the wild emotions it brings, is part of the process. This kind of training is negated when commanders themselves encourage war crimes, as is conspicuous with Russia's Ukraine invasion. In the first weeks of invasion, Russian television celebrated the systematic looting of captured towns. Russian soldiers were shown filing into post offices to mail home stolen televisions and computers and anything else they could loot. Ukrainian drone operators were at first puzzled by the sight of objects resembling washing machines strapped to the hulls of Russian tanks. Then they realised they *were* in fact washing machines, looted from captured towns. The horrors at Bucha were not just the result of lack of discipline among the troops, but of orders from above. Training and education has no effect when an invading power specifically condones its troops' barbarity. No screening of likely war criminals is possible when an entire army is encouraged to commit atrocities.

Better understanding of who commits war crimes and why they do it will help prevent those crimes in the future. That knowledge is already having an effect, as in the training of UN peacekeepers.

❭ ❭ ❭ ❭ ❭ ❭

One of the most effective measures against war crimes is likely to be the least spectacular, and the hardest to measure. That is the cumulative effect of a web of treaties and laws stretching beyond war crimes. Restrictions on money laundering, arms trading and commodity smuggling will limit operations for the armed bands across the world who commit many of its atrocities.

Convincing governments to give more support for war crimes justice will depend on explaining what it is for. Righting wrongs, of course. But the ICC can also provide tangible benefits. For the wider world, small wars are expensive to clean up afterwards. There are peacekeepers to pay for, and aid, and rebuilding shattered towns. The cost of these humanitarian programmes runs into the billions. A compelling argument for the bean counters is that if war crimes courts are effective enough to be feared, warlords will think twice before going to war in the first place.

Added to that is the concept of staying the hand of vengeance. This is the title of a book by war crimes expert Gary Bass, which points out that trials offer an alternative to revenge. It was a key objective of the UN's Yugoslavia tribunal to jail the leaders of ethnic cleansing. Letting them walk free would invite a war of revenge by their former victims.

Equally important is to provide a historical record of who did what to whom. In both Bosnia and Rwanda, massacres were rationalised as being revenge for previous imagined hurts. War crimes trials provide a solid record of what actually happened, with the hope of stopping future extremists twisting the truth.

The desire to leave a record has led war crimes courts into choppy waters. The high point of the Yugoslavia tribunal was supposed to be the trial of former Serbian president Slobodan Milošević. He was the architect of a string of wars in Croatia, then Bosnia, and later Kosovo. The tribunal decided to try him for all three, reasoning that crimes needed to be accounted for. The result was a four-year trial that had yet to finish when Milošević died of heart failure. Future trials may do better to avoid the time and cost of such long processes, and concentrate instead simply on finding enough evidence to convict. A prime example of such pragmatism was the famous case of the FBI jailing gangster boss Al Capone for tax evasion. Unable to find witnesses willing to testify to his more gruesome crimes, they realised he had filed no tax returns to explain his lavish spending. In the end, prosecutors were happy enough just to have him behind bars.

In the foreseeable future, it is unlikely the ICC will be given further powers. If it is to be more effective, it will be by making more use of the powers it already has. That will be true in one particular area: the option, never yet used, to prosecute not just generals and warlords but the banks and corporations who enable them.

Follow the Money

Out of the 100 richest entities in the world, 69 are not countries but businesses.* Globalisation means transnational corporations girdle the world. Apple has higher revenues than Belgium, BP is richer than Switzerland. The combined revenue of the ten biggest transnational corporations is $285 trillion, more than the combined wealth of 180 of the world's 193 nations. Yet war crimes law concentrates only on states. The ICC has never indicted a corporation. This is despite the UN reporting that 40 per cent of modern wars are motivated by finance, and most of the rest have a business component. Arms dealers

---

* Source: Global Justice Now report, based on figures from CIA World Factbook and Future Global 500.

sell weapons, mining giants take diamonds and gold from captured territory.

Not all transnational corporations commit war crimes, but those that do mostly escape censure. In Guatemala, troops enforce violent evictions to clear vast areas for foreign-owned plantations. Papua New Guinea's rainforest is being devastated and its indigenous people persecuted to clear land for palm oil corporations. Cambodia's Khmer Rouge regime, one of the most violent in history, prospered through a logging trade worth $90 million a year with corporations based in Thailand. More recently, Islamic State's hold on portions of Iraq and Syria was financed by oil sales to foreign companies.

Laws already exist to allow the ICC to indict a corporate chief for war crimes. In the beginning, that was the intention. Its first prosecutor, Louis Moreno Ocampo, announced it as a priority soon after being appointed in 2003. At a corporate lawyers' conference in San Francisco that year he warned he would soon be coming after some of their bosses. 'He got serious by linking mass killings in the Democratic Republic of Congo to the world of business law,' recorded the breathless official report of the speech. 'He intends to investigate the companies to ascertain whether any of them should be brought before the ICC.'

Ocampo confirmed his intention later that year at the ICC's annual conference, again focusing on Congo: 'Those who direct mining operations, sell diamonds or gold extracted in these conditions, launder the dirty money or provide weapons could also be authors of the crimes. Even if they are based in other countries.'

Legally, Ocampo had the ammunition. 'Follow the trail of money and you will find the criminals,' he told the BBC that year. Ocampo chose Congo for three reasons. First, its war remains the worst anywhere since the Second World War. For five years it was the centre of the Great War of Africa, involving armies from five outside nations as well as a myriad of local armed groups. More than 2.5 million died in the war, many from disease and starvation, in fighting that raged over a country the size of Western Europe. That is a higher toll than Afghanistan, Bosnia, Iraq and Vietnam combined. The war formally ended in 2003, but it continues in eastern Congo to this day with a litany of terror, rape and massacres.

Second was that DRC had given the ICC jurisdiction, and third was that its wars are fought for plunder. Plunder is not new to Congo. In fact, the country was formed for that specific purpose.

❯ ❯ ❯ ❯ ❯ ❯

King Leopold II of Belgium claimed the territory that is now the DRC in 1885, during Europe's Scramble for Africa. And not for Belgium, but for himself personally, lured by big profits to be made from ivory, timber, and most of all rubber. Rubber was in high demand in Europe and America, used in tyres for the new bicycles that were being churned out. Scottish inventor John Boyd Dunlop was already working on his revolutionary pneumatic tyre.

To the outside world Leopold promised his Congo Free State would be run for the benefit of the population, a radical change from the exploitation carried out in European empires. There would be fair trade, profits for all. The reality was different.

He set up trading posts along the long winding Congo river, and established a capital city near the coast. But the rubber produced by villagers was far less than he needed to break even.

One reason was that rubber harvesting in Congo was difficult and unpleasant. Rubber comes from vines, which have to be drained to release it. Lacking technology, the only practical way for villages to do this was cut open the vine, then slather their bodies with the liquid. They then waited for it to dry, and someone else hacked it off. The process was long, and also painful, as clumps of hair would be torn off with the rubber. Hence, local farmers kept production to a minimum. They produced enough to pay for essentials and left it at that.

Leopold, facing ruinous losses, determined to change their minds. He unleashed his private army, Force Publique, to terrorise the inhabitants to harvest more rubber. Villages were burned, populations massacred, and Force Publique cut off the hands of farmers deemed not to be working ;hard enough. Soldiers took to wearing necklaces made of human ears, to prove to officers that they were enthusiastic enforcers. Mayhem swept the Free State. Tens of thousands fled their homes. Thousands more starved, as their rubber work left crops neglected. The upheavals triggered epidemics of sleeping sickness, smallpox and dysentery.

The man who first blew the whistle was an African American Baptist minister, George Washington Williams. A veteran of the Civil War, and later the first African American elected to the Ohio legislature, Williams made a name for himself as a human rights advocate, writing on the evils of American slavery. He is credited with inventing the term 'crimes against humanity' to describe slavery's degradations. In 1889 he journeyed up the Congo River, then sent a despatch detailing the horrors: 'Your Majesty's Government has sequestered their land, burned their towns, stolen their property, enslaved their women and children, and committed other crimes too numerous to mention in detail.'[†]

⊦ ⧽ ▶ ▶ ▶ ▶

That same year, Joseph Conrad skippered a steamer up the river, writing of the barbarism in his acclaimed *Heart of Darkness.* Arthur Conan Doyle paused his Sherlock Holmes novels to pen an angry call to arms, *The Crime of the Congo,* writing: 'The crime which has been wrought in the Congo lands by King Leopold of Belgium and his followers to be the greatest which has ever been known in human annals.'

More evidence of the horrors emerged in the photographs taken by British missionary, Alice Seeley Harris. One picture, reprinted in Europe and America, showed a farmer kneeling in front of the tiny severed hands of his five-year-old daughter. She had been mutilated by soldiers of the Anglo-Belgian Rubber Company.

Belgium could have prosecuted Leopold and the corporations involved. It had the laws in place but instead, in 1908, it contented itself with taking formal control of the colony away from the king. Independence from

† Williams, George Washington, 'Open Letter to King Leopold On The Congo' (2023) www.blackpast.org

Belgium came in June 1960, followed by civil war. By then, the world's demands had moved to copper, and fierce fighting broke out in the mining areas of Katanga. The war drew in mercenaries, Belgian forces and revolutionary leader Che Guevara. Politically it was baffling, but commercially very simple. Everyone wanted Congo's copper, along with its gold and diamonds. A Belgian corporation funded a mercenary brigade led by 'Mad' Mike Hoare. Hoare, a former British army officer, who became a template for the morally ambiguous mercenary. He led a brigade that liberated a northern capital, Stanleyville, securing its mining areas. The motif of Hoare's unit was a picture of wild geese, an image later immortalised in a film of the same name. Among the war's casualties was the UN Secretary General, Dag Hammarskjold. He arrived in 1961 to try and mediate, but died in a plane crash. Investigations never established if this was accidental or deliberate.

The war ended in 1965 when a US-backed general, Mobutu Seso Seko, captured the capital. Mobutu cancelled democracy and changed the country's name to Zaire. Then, like Leopold, ran the country for his personal enrichment. Mobutu is conservatively estimated to have stashed at least four billion dollars abroad, mostly in Swiss banks, earned from the mining trade. He was ousted in 1997 by an army officer, Laurent-Désiré Kabila, who changed the country's name back to Democratic Republic of Congo. A year later war broke out anew, and this time it was huge. Congo's civil war became known as the Great War of Africa because it sucked in armies from Rwanda and Uganda in the east, and Angola, Namibia and Zimbabwe in the south and west. Once again, plunder was the objective.

By now, the outside world was in the grip of a technological revolution. Computers and phones were in every home. Congo was once more in a position to provide. It has vast reserves of gold, and of three metals, tantalum, tin and tungsten, used in every computer on the planet. In eastern Congo, Rwandan and Ugandan forces took direct control of the mines, shipping product throughout their countries to grateful corporations. The course of the war evolved into a template: armed groups captured mines, then enslaved local people to mine them. This enslavement was accompanied by murder, rape and torture. One unique horror unfolded at the Gorumbwa gold mine.

Gorumbwa sits in a bend in the Kibali River, surrounded by lush, forested hills. It was seized by Ugandan troops early in the war, but they were left with a problem. Most mining in Congo is alluvial. That is, on the surface. Rock and soil are broken or sifted to extract the metals. But Gorumbwa was deep underground. There were shafts and tunnels to reach the gold seams. When the mine was seized, many engineers fled. That left the soldiers unable to operate the equipment or obtain spare parts. Their solution was to use forced labour. Local villagers were rounded up at gunpoint. Army explosives were used to blast the caverns underground, then the labourers were used to hack out the gold.

This gunpoint mining saw executions and punishment beatings for those accused of not working hard enough. Just over one tonne of gold was mined in the first year, but commanders wanted more. They started blasting underground pillars left in place to hold up tunnel ceilings. One morning, the inevitable happened and the mine caved in. More than one hundred forced workers were trapped underground. They remain there still.

The disaster was highlighted by Human Rights Watch in a seminal report, *The Curse of Gold*. It records the dismay of a local engineer. 'The Ugandan army were responsible for the destruction of Gorumbwa mine. It was not their country so they didn't care about the destruction.'

Even after a UN peace plan officially ended the Great War of Africa in 2003, fighting continued. Although the foreign armies withdrew, their proxy forces continued the struggle. Sometimes mines are captured to fund the fighting, sometimes their capture is the reason for the fighting.

For more than a century, Congo has provided the world with timber, rubber, ivory, diamonds, copper, gold and rare metals. Its population have gained little in return. In 2021, the UN Human Development Index ranked the population as twelfth poorest on the planet. And in all this time, no corporation was ever prosecuted for any of it. It was not for lack of evidence. Information on mining abuses in Congo has been pouring in ever since. The same year Ocampo made his fiery speech, the United Nations produced a report accusing eighty-five foreign companies of benefiting from DRC's illicit mineral trade. That list was later whittled down, but the UN's panel of experts, who compiled the report, urged their masters to sanction twenty-nine firms. Among the big hitters accused were Anglo American, Barclays Bank, Bayer and South Africa's De Beers. No sanctions were issued on any of them.

A year later, a nuts-and-bolts study of how the ICC could try corporations linked to war crimes

perpetrated in Congo was published by law expert
Julia Graff of American University Washington
College of Law. Her paper underlined that you don't
have to wear a uniform to commit war crimes. Or
be charged for them. The test is whether you had
some control, or aided those who did. Graff walked
through each step of the process, providing almost a
blueprint for an investigation. And showed it could
be done.

A year after that, the Gorumbwa mine disaster and
much else was exposed by Human Rights Watch. Its
Curse of Gold report was a doorstopper, packed with
evidence. Another NGO, Global Witness, produced
reports highlighting links between corporations and
militias. Then in 2010, yet more evidence came, via
the US Congress. Congress passed the Wall Street
Reform Act, designed to try and stop a repeat of the
banking crash of 2008. Tucked away in its provisions
were requirements for corporations to explain which
Congo mines they got their material from.

The law has seen only patchy enforcement ever
since, but the background information was yet more
evidence for war crimes prosecutors. Congress, the
UN, Human Rights Watch and Global Witness were
basically doing the ICC's job for it. All it needed was
a criminal case.

The reasons it never happened are hotly disputed. Ocampo's defenders say he lacked the resources to go after the mining corporations while also opening investigations into a dozen countries and simultaneously setting up the prosecutor's office in the new court. Ocampo himself never went into the reasons. Stepping down at the end of his nine-year term, he admitted indicting corporate bosses was difficult. 'It won't be easy. We need time.'

Like war law itself, indicting a corporate or banking executive for war crimes is simple in theory. Underpinning war crimes prosecutions is the idea of aiming for the top. Indicting warlords is preferable to indicting their soldiers because otherwise it leaves warlords free to recruit new soldiers. The same logic holds for going after corporate bosses. It is no use limiting prosecutions to the warlords and generals sponsored by corporations, if those corporations are free to hire willing replacements.

The crucial distinction is not whether a suspect has a military rank, but whether they have control over units that are committing atrocities. This might be as an army commander, or it might be through delivering weapons, or taking delivery of plundered metals. In legalese, the crucial phrase is 'de facto'. A corporate boss in an air-conditioned office in Europe may not have direct control over the day-to-day operations of the militias bringing him his product, but as the paymaster he has a de facto command position.

While no international court has ever jailed a corporate executive, the same procedure was used for the stand-out war crimes conviction of modern times. It was the only conviction in recent years of a former head of state, and in fact only the second time a former head of state has ever been convicted of war crimes by an international court. (The first was Germany's Karl Dönitz, who took over from Hitler in the last days of the German Reich and was jailed at Nuremberg.)

꘏ ꘏ ꘏ ꘏ ꘏ ꘏

The second conviction was of former Liberian president Charles Taylor. Taylor was president of Liberia through much of the 1990s, but made his fortune supporting savage militias who plundered the diamond fields neighbouring Sierra Leone. These blood diamonds are among the purest in the world, and Taylor grew immensely rich selling them to the world market. To get the diamonds, the rebels he armed and financed terrorised the mining regions. Thousands were murdered, tortured and enslaved. Then the diamonds were smuggled to him across the border.

Taylor was tried at the Sierra Leone Special Court, a joint operation between Sierra Leone's government and the UN. His four-year trial ended in conviction and a fifty-year jail sentence, the longest ever imposed for war crimes. Missed at the time by many commentators was the fact that due to a legal complication he was not convicted for ordering those war crimes, but instead for aiding and abetting. Taylor had never set foot in Sierra Leone. He had never commanded the rebel units that committed the horrific crimes and plundered the diamonds. Instead, he was jailed for financing and enabling them.

This legal process can be used against corporate bosses supporting war crimes in return for profit. His conviction highlighted that you don't have to order war crimes to be convicted of them. You don't even need to be in the same country.

However, Taylor's prosecution came with a problem and that same problem will confront future aiding and abetting prosecutions In their efforts to fix that problem, Taylor's prosecutors summoned one of the most unlikely witnesses in war crimes history.

Naomi Campbell's Diamonds

Almost everyone in the world knew the name of the witness who took the stand one day in August 2010 wearing a figure-hugging cream dress. Supermodel Naomi Campbell started out by explaining she was testifying under duress. 'I didn't really want to be here, I was made to be here.' Campbell had been subpoenaed to testify about the night she met Charles Taylor, at a dinner in 1997 thrown by South African president Nelson Mandela.

The dinner featured half a dozen international celebrities and one murderous tyrant. Why Mandela, lauded as the bringer of peace to South Africa, had included Taylor on his guest list was a mystery unanswered in court testimony. The dinner finished and the guests went to bed in villas in Mandela's presidential compound. Campbell was asleep when there was a knock at her door.

'I opened my door and two men were there and gave me a pouch and said "a gift for you".'

Inside the pouch were some small hard rocks. 'They were kind of dirty looking pebbles,' she explained.

In fact, they were uncut diamonds, part of Taylor's vast haul stolen from Sierra Leone. He had brought them to sell in South Africa, and had enough extra to give to the supermodel. Campbell said she was not sure at the time that they were diamonds: 'I'm used to seeing diamonds shiny and in a box,' she told the court.

Proof that they were indeed uncut diamonds came later, when the man she gave them to, the head of a charity, was arrested by South African police for keeping them in his safe. Ironically, the law against holding unregistered diamonds was a result of the blood diamonds legislation drawn up in response to Taylor's operation.

꘎ ꘎ ꘎ ꘎ ꘎ ꘎

Campbell wasn't the only one wondering why she was in court that day. She knew nothing of Taylor before meeting him, and never saw him again. Nor did she even speak to him at the dinner. Critics of the trial said prosecutors had summoned her as a publicity stunt. That may have played a part in their decision, but the main reason was that they had a problem with the case. They had plenty of evidence of horrific war crimes, and plenty also that Taylor had made hundreds of millions of dollars from the plundered diamonds. What they were missing was the piece in the middle, proving that he knew of the horrors meted out in order to get them.

The problem was command responsibility. In war law, a commander is responsible for the actions of their troops. That is articulated in the ICC's Article 28, which says command responsibility means just what it says. Commanders are responsible for the crimes even if they did not order them. It is enough that the crimes were widespread, and that the commander failed to either prevent or punish them. Crucially, that is the case even if there is no proof that the commander knew they were happening. The reasoning is that, while a commander might not know everything that is happening on a battlefield, they should know about systematic crimes. The key phrase is that they are guilty because they 'should have known' the crimes were happening.

But the rules of aiding and abetting are different. In the case of Charles Taylor, as in the case of a corporate boss, ignorance is a defence. To jail Taylor, prosecutors had to prove he knew. In court the test for this is strict. It is not enough to argue that the defendant must have known, it has to be proven to be true.

That was the piece of the jigsaw that Campbell was summoned to provide: it proved Taylor was handling uncut diamonds, giving the lie to his claim on trial that he had never possessed an uncut diamond in his life.

The other pieces of the jigsaw came from a quirk of the Sierra Leone Special Court that may become a future template. When the court was set up, money was tight. The total cost was $300 million, so its bosses cut their coat according to their cloth. They decreed that only the topmost leaders of the war would go to trial. Everyone else would be offered the alternative of a truth and reconciliation commission. They would gain immunity for all the crimes they confessed to, provided they committed no more.

The commission had a cathartic effect on the country, but it produced something else too. Among those confessing were the deputies to the leaders on trial. They provided vital inside knowledge that prosecutors could use. In the case of Taylor, those confessors were priceless. Prosecutors had access to witnesses who had been in the room when Taylor made his decisions.

Witnesses who testified that Taylor knew about the horrors his operation was inflicting.

If the ICC prosecutes corporate and banking chiefs, they could take a leaf out of the Sierra Leone court's book and offer amnesties in return for evidence to their deputies.

Even without inside information, there are other ways to prove a chief executive knew about the wars they financed. Company documents are the obvious route. But so too are human rights reports. It is one reason for the apparently redundant practice of rights groups taking pains to record the delivery of their reports to officials. A company boss might deny reading those reports otherwise.

Going after corporations has other advantages for the ICC. For one thing, corporate chiefs are easy to arrest. They live in modern cities and have no armies to protect them. A few prominent prosecutions may also have an outsized effect on corporate crimes worldwide. That is down to how the court works. It doesn't indict entities or corporations, but only individuals. Its argument is that people, not organisations, make decisions. This may prove a more powerful deterrent than prosecuting a company. As a chain of civil suits against corporations for rights violations and pollution have shown, corporations can shrug off fines. But a prison sentence is something a chief executive is going to take seriously.

If the ICC does go down that road, however, it can expect to meet serious political opposition. The fact that those 69 corporations are among the world's 100 richest entities highlights their political punch. A punch that makes governments uncomfortable. Politicians depend on corporations for political donations, and many politicians are invited to sit on company boards. Debate rages over just how powerful transnational corporations truly are. They are often able to bend governments to their will, for example shopping around for the cheapest tax deal when choosing which country to be based in. But the corporations are also in competition with each other. Indictments against corporate chiefs will likely be welcomed by the boardrooms of the competition, for giving them a new gap in the market.

Nevertheless, pushback against indicting corporate chiefs is likely from the ICC member nations. Lobbyists will urge politicians to remember the economy. How much that would affect the prosecutions is unclear. The ICC member states set the rules, but they have no day-to-day control of the court. Chief prosecutors have set nine-year terms, and firing one because they wanted to investigate big business would see a public opinion backlash. So would any change of the court's rules that prohibited going after the members of boardrooms. Yet prosecutors would face the reality of knowing many member states would be hostile, and most obviously would vote against any budget increases for the court. It would be making enemies, just as it was seeking to make new friends.

It feels necessary to mention the potential backlash, to underline that targeting some corporate chiefs would be a political, rather than a legal decision. As the Taylor case proved, there are no legal obstacles to target all who facilitate war crimes, whether in battlefields or boardrooms. Whether the ICC's future involves corporate prosecutions is up to the prosecutor. There is nothing collegiate about the ICC's office of the prosecutor. The big decisions are all made by the chief. Since 2021, that chief has been Karim Khan. So will he take the plunge?

Personal disclosure: I know him a little. He assisted me with my first war crimes book, a fact that clouds objective assessment. One thing friends and critics agree on is that he is combative, having made his bones as a high-profile war crimes defence lawyer, defending Taylor and once staging a theatrical walkout – at which the judge told him, 'Mr Khan, you have not been given leave to withdraw. You don't just get up and waltz out of here.'

Later, he defended Kenya's deputy president, accused of responsibility for violence following elections in 2007 that left 1,200 dead. The court later dropped charges of murder, deportation and persecution because of a lack of evidence. But in a split ruling, one of the judges said it was a mistrial became of 'a troubling incidence of witness interference and intolerable political meddling'. That interference included the murder of a prosecution witness. Kenyan rights groups accused Khan of ignoring the interference and of witness intimidation, a charge he rejected. In an open letter he wrote: 'Four Kenyan NGOs attempt to create a spectre against me in this election process.' Instead, he said, he had acted to request protection for the murdered witness after hearing of threats.

Khan was not on the original shortlist of prosecutor candidates, and was added after lobbying from several states, including Kenya and Britain. Supporters say his long experience in defence makes him an ideal prosecutor, a 'poacher turned gamekeeper' who knows all the tricks. He certainly knows the law, having authored one of the key reference books on war crimes statutes.

Also in his favour is a pugnacious attitude. In office, he slimmed down the caseload, the first ICC prosecutor ever to end cases, with the dropping of investigations into Afghanistan and the Central African Republic to save money. For the Putin case, he selected as lead prosecutor American Brenda Hollis, who has a stellar reputation. She was the lead prosecutor against Taylor, and is known, as is Khan, to have a steely personality.

His decision with the Ukraine case to start at the top, by indicting Putin, indicates boldness. The fact that Putin will probably never stand trial will not enhance the court's reputation, but avoiding the indictment of Russia's commander-in-chief would have shown weakness. Khan can justifiably claim that his job is to go after those responsible, while others have the problem of bringing them to trial. Whether he takes the same attitude with corporate chiefs involved in war crimes is not clear. He made no mention of it, or any other investigations, in his acceptance speech in 2021. In apparent acknow-ledgement of the failure of the court to make an impact in its first two decades, he said: 'We cannot invest so much, we cannot raise expectations so high and achieve so little, so often in the courtroom.'

One clue to his strategy is his emphasis on cooperating with the governments of states he is investigating. In one way, that is in line with the ideology of the ICC. It is a court set up to operate only when member states cannot, or will not, prosecute themselves. Ukraine is a prime example: it is holding its own war crimes cases parallel to the ICC, but Kyiv has asked the ICC to take on the bigger indictments because Ukraine's resources are limited.

However, cooperation with the governments the court is supposed to be investigating is an obvious conflict of interest. Defence lawyers before Khan came to office criticised the previous prosecutors for signing memorandums of understanding with the same states they were supposed to be investigating. Some will worry that cooperation effectively gives governments a free pass when indictments are handed out.

Khan himself said in his opening speech that 'the proof of the pudding is in the eating', and what will count will be convictions. He has the boldness to take on corporations, but it is unclear yet whether he also has the inclination. Going after corporate, as well as military, war criminals would expand the ICC's brief, but it would also run into the same problem that crimps all its operations – its lack of reach. Barring a rare UN referral, the ICC is limited to prosecuting crimes only in member states. There is, however, another justice mechanism in play.

The Cinderellas

There are two kinds of war crimes justice. International trials grab most of the headlines, but an equally potent system exists in national courts. More than two dozen countries have some form of universal jurisdiction legislation. That allows courts to prosecute war crimes even if neither the crime nor the perpetrator is linked to that country. These are the Cinderellas of international justice. Most of the time they are invisible, but when they go to the ball, everyone notices.

That's what happened one dull autumn day in London in 1998. Few paid much attention to the slightly stooped eighty-two-year-old man who arrived at one of London's most discreet private hospitals. London Bridge Hospital is a low brick building on the banks of the Thames. Anonymous outside, home to some of the world's top surgeons on the inside.

The man had flown halfway around the world to be there, to have some minor back surgery. But at least one person was watching, because this was no ordinary patient. He was General Augusto Pinochet, once the great and terrible dictator of Chile.

Pinochet smashed his way to power in 1973. He led an army coup against the elected president, Salvador Allende. Tanks and planes hammered the presidential palace, and when troops stormed in, they found Allende's body in the rubble.

What followed was a seventeen-year reign of terror. The army rounded up students, politicians, lawyers, anybody who might disagree with soldiers running the country. They caught so many in the first week that the jails were full, and they shunted them into the national football stadium. Some were jailed, a few released, and many were never seen again. Outside the capital, an army death squad dubbed the Caravan of Death roamed the country. Political opponents, friends of those opponents, potential opponents or simply people in the wrong place at the wrong time were hauled into the net. Some were tortured, some shot, and some bundled into helicopters, flown out over the sea and thrown out alive.

Resistance was futile, but some tried it anyway. The wives and mothers of the disappeared began meeting each week in town squares. Then they would dance by themselves, holding a picture of their loved one. The ritual was later memorialised in Sting's haunting song, 'They Dance Alone'.

Pinochet fell in 1990, part of the wave of democracy then sweeping the world. And like many dictators, he cut a deal. In exchange for going quietly, he negotiated a lifetime immunity agreement. At least, in Chilean law.

But other eyes were watching. Spain is one of about two dozen states that have universal jurisdiction laws, and in Spanish law, murdering a Spanish citizen is a crime wherever it happens. And in Chile, in 1973, more than a hundred Spanish citizens had been killed and many more tortured.

The obvious problem with universal jurisdiction is how to reach the perpetrator. Pinochet sensed Spain would be a problem, so he would not be seeking medical treatment there. London seemed a safer bet, partly because he was friends with Margaret Thatcher. She was prime minister during the Falklands War, and the two had made common cause against Argentina. Pinochet gave Britain help and Thatcher was grateful. She would invite him to tea during his regular London visits.

This visit was different. Once he was confirmed to have arrived, Spain issued an extradition warrant. And British police served it on the general as he lay recuperating in hospital one Friday night.

The case was a sensation. Pinochet never dreamed that a court in one country could get police in a second country to arrest a man for crimes committed in a third country. But now he knew different. His case dragged along for eighteen months, finally reaching the House of Lords, at the time the UK's supreme court. And there, in a decision that sent shockwaves around the world, the Law Lords ruled that for the most serious crimes, there is no immunity. Even for ex-presidents.

In the end it didn't matter, because politics stepped in. The government of Tony Blair had come to power the year before, proclaiming their 'ethical foreign policy'. The Pinochet case was the first casualty. Anxious about upsetting trading partners, and possibly other ex-dictators, the government overruled the lords and sent Pinochet home. Officially, he was declared too sick to stand trial. The decision became even more controversial after Pinochet arrived home, was wheeled off his plane in a wheelchair, but then stood up, showing he remained sprightly. It was a defeat for Spain, but the point was made. The potential of universal jurisdiction had been revealed.

In one way, universal jurisdiction is a contradiction in terms. The UN Charter, signed by all member states, lays heavy emphasis on states being able to do what they want in their own backyard. But the UN's Universal Declaration of Human Rights, the most widely accepted rights treaty, emphasises rights all citizens of the world should enjoy. The declaration was created soon after the UN was formed, drafted by a commission headed by Eleanor Roosevelt, widow of the former US president. It opens by declaring: 'Equal and inalienable rights of all members of the human family is the foundation of freedom, justice and peace in the world.'

One difference between the UN Charter and the Universal Declaration of Human Rights is that the Charter is a legal document, while the Universal Declaration is non-binding. Another is that all UN members have to sign the Charter to join the UN, whereas the declaration is optional. All states have signed some of the treaties that arose from it, but many have not signed all of them. The Charter also declares the importance of human rights, but states are not compelled to take notice.

The Universal Declaration of Human Rights turned from an aspiration to a legal document in 1976, with a treaty named the International Covenant on Civil and

Political Rights. Even then, the long lists of rights proclaimed had no enforcement mechanism. As Dunant and Lemkin found with their Geneva and Genocide Conventions, persuading states to sign up is one thing. Ensuring that they enforce the provisions is something else. As the 2003 Iraq invasion showed, declaring an act illegal is pointless if there is no court to enforce it.

The architects of universal jurisdiction turned that logic on its head. Sure, there is nothing that compels states to obey all those human rights treaties they sign. Equally, there is nothing to stop other states enforcing them. In Pinochet's case, he had signed the Torture Convention, making torture illegal under Chilean law. All the Spanish prosecutor was doing was taking Chile at its word. The convention declared torture a universal crime so, in effect, Spain was simply following rules Chile had signed up to.

One effect of the Pinochet affair was to put retired presidents on notice. In 2011, former US president George W. Bush cancelled plans to visit Switzerland, amid rumours that three arrest warrants awaited him. All were supposedly from other, unnamed states who practise universal jurisdiction. Their focus was the US military prison at Guantánamo Bay. In the event, Bush cancelled the trip, and details of the warrants were never made public. Rights groups celebrated the shudder that went through ex-presidents, as those with skeletons in the closet realised secret indictments might be waiting for them at foreign airports.

And not just ex-presidents. Syrian torturer Anwar Raslan found out the reach of universal jurisdiction the hard way. When the Syrian civil war began in 2011, Raslan operated a notorious prison under the aegis of Bashar al-Assad, kidnapping and torturing opponents. More than 4,000 were tortured and at least 58 murdered, in a sadistic regime featuring beatings, rapes, mutilation and electric shock torture.

Tiring of his work, Raslan later fled to Germany, hiding among the mass exodus of Syrian refugees. He settled with his family into a comfortable life in Berlin, his past forgotten. Then one day one of his former victims recognised him on the street. The victim told a rights group and they told the police. His trial featured grim evidence: one former victim described being hung by his wrists from the ceiling, while a gravedigger recalled hundreds of bodies, some badly mutilated, being thrown into mass graves. In 2022 Raslan was jailed for life for crimes against humanity.

The pace of universal jurisdiction cases is growing. There were 815 such cases around the world in the decade ending in 2017, which is double the average number of cases in each of the two decades before. In 2021, there were a record 125 cases, spread across sixteen countries‡ in just that twelve-month period. The laws to allow such proceedings have been around for many years. What has changed is the appetite of prosecutors to use them.

Some of those laws go back a long way. America's Aliens Tort Claims Act dates from 1789, when it was made to deal with pirates on the high seas. It allows lawsuits when neither the victim nor the protagonist are American. Until 1980, only two cases were ever brought. Since then, there has been a flood. Among them, in 2007, Yahoo paid compensation to dissidents tortured by China after Beijing tracked them through the internet. In 2019, Belgium jailed two businessmen for exporting sarin gas components to Syria. Oil giant Shell paid compensation to Nigerian farmers for despoiling their land.

Most current universal jurisdiction cases have been brought in Europe, including Spain, Germany, France, Switzerland, the Netherlands and the Nordic countries. But universal jurisdiction is gathering pace elsewhere. Senegal authorised the setting up of a hybrid court, sharing control with the UN, to

‡ Maximo Lange, University of California, quoted in *The Economist*.

jail Chad's former president Hissène Habré for mass murder. Like Raslan, Habre had fled into exile in Senegal assuming he was safe from prosecution.

What gives universal jurisdiction teeth is that it can reach parts of the world the ICC cannot. It has become a powerful tool in the United States, despite its own reluctance to join the ICC. In 2022, one of the most extraordinary judgments saw a French construction giant, Lafarge, pay a $778 million fine to a US court after admitting it had financed war crimes in Syria.

Lafarge built a $680 million cement plant in northern Syria shortly before the outbreak of civil war. When violence broke out, it sought to protect its investment, keeping the plant going. When ISIS captured the region, court documents show it giving $6 million to the terrorist group to keep the plant working and earn $70 million. 'The terrorism crimes to which Lafarge and its subsidiary have pleaded guilty are a vivid reminder of how corporate crime can intersect with national security,' said America's deputy attorney general, Lisa O. Monaco.

America brought the prosecution because Lafarge has a presence in the United States. Following its guilty plea, French prosecutors have begun their own case against Lafarge chiefs.

In September 2023, in what may become a landmark case, Sweden begins the prosecution of the chairman and of the former chief executive officer of its biggest oil company, Lundin Energy. Both are charged with aiding war crimes in Sudan. Unlike America's Lafarge case, the charges are against the bosses personally, not the company. If found guilty, they face jail. The case, however it turns out, will likely mark the first time since the Nuremberg trials that a major company boss is prosecuted for war crimes.

Not everyone is happy. Former US Secretary of State Henry Kissinger, criticised for his support of Pinochet's coup, has complained that universal jurisdiction threatens a new kind of tyranny. His fear is that it gives power to unelected judges to run the world, with the risk that law is arbitrary.

How tyrannical, or otherwise, the world's judges become is a separate issue from the potency of these laws. The key thing about universal jurisdiction is that laws to make it happen have been around for decades. They were created each time a human rights convention was signed, albeit by states who never dreamed that one day they would be held to account. The Pinochet case was for that reason a clarion call for the possibilities of reviving long-neglected laws. Critics complain that many cases are tried because a prosecutor wants to make a name for themselves with a splashy verdict. Yet this may be no bad thing. The prosecutor is not the judge or jury; their job is to dig out evidence. Personal ambition is a fine driving force, if it means criminals are brought to account.

If war crimes future ends up being more potent than war crimes past, it will likely be with national and international courts working in parallel. National courts have more reach than the ICC, in that they can prosecute crimes anywhere in the world. They can also have more powers to try corporate cases. The ICC will likely be restricted in issuing subpoenas to look inside a company files for evidence it knew of war crimes it was sponsoring. National courts will have no such problems, especially if they couple a war crimes investigation with probes for bribery and tax evasion. Those are more likely to allow a comprehensive examination of company files in the search for evidence.

All of which gives national prosecutors formidable powers to investigate corporations involved in war crimes. As with the ICC, the laws to do so are already in place. What will matter in the future is the boldness of prosecutors.

American Canary

In the summer of 2003 bunkers appeared on the sandy beaches of The Hague. They were the work not of an army but of human rights activists. Digging them was a symbolic protest against an American law enabling US forces to storm the jail of the International Criminal Court.

That law, the American Service Members Protection Act, is the toughest in a raft of measures successive US governments have taken to crimp the powers of the ICC. Dubbed by opponents the Hague Invasion Act, it gives the president the power to send forces to free US citizens held on ICC charges. In theory, those powers include sending Marines to storm the Dutch beaches, hence the symbolic bunkers. And not just Dutch ones. The law allows the same action in any country in the world.

No country agonises over war crimes justice like the United States. Possibly this is linked to how the USA was formed. Most countries are simply gatherings of a national group. Not America. It was founded on an ideal. Against that, American exceptionalism is a strong current across its political spectrum. The USA's political class manages to be both internationalist and isolationist at the same time. Leader of the Free World, yet also apart from it.

Whatever the reasons, America has been both the greatest friend and the greatest foe of war crimes justice. It was the country that made the General Orders 100, the first modern war crimes law, which later became the Hague Convention. It gave homes to immigrants Lieber and Lemkin, both buried in New York City. Andrew Carnegie, having made millions building America's railroads, financed the world's first purpose-built war crimes court. Even the procedures of war crimes courts borrow heavily from the US's adversarial system. The UN courts and the ICC use the adversarial system, in which prosecution and defence fight it out, with judges acting as referees. The alternative would have been the inquisitorial system, where the judge functions as chief investigator, questioning witnesses to find the truth. Antonio Cassese, first president of the ICTY, said one reason as to why so much of the US system was heavily adopted was because Albright had provided free legal experts in the early days when the UN itself would not. The ICC has in turn borrowed procedures from the UN courts. An exception being the judge's robes. Cassese, a charismatic Florentine, decreed that UN judges should wear red robes, while ICC judicial robes are blue. And yet America remains aloof from a system it did so much to create.

In the 1990s, the Clinton administration agonised like no other over whether to intervene in Bosnia. As chronicled in Samantha Power's *A Problem from Hell*, Clinton officials were torn between wanting to stop the horrors in the Balkans and fearing any US peacekeepers sent in would end up in a Vietnam-style quagmire. In the end, no peacekeepers were sent, though America later hosted the Bosnia peace conference in Dayton, Ohio.

Plenty of states oppose the ICC, but America is until now the only one to take active measures against it. Those measures began as soon as the court started work. As well as the invasion act, the Bush administration began aggressively demanding immunity from the court from member states. Washington did this after realising the ICC had a chink in its armour.

That chink is Article 98 of the statute. This allows member states to cut their own immunity deals. Article 98 gives any state the power to give nationals of any other state immunity from arrest under ICC warrant. The Bush administration put diplomatic pressure on dozens of ICC members to sign agreements, threatening that otherwise aid payments would be cut. Aid was indeed cut to three nations that refused such deals: Kenya, South Africa and Tanzania. In the end 102 states signed immunity deals. Some of those states did it even though they were not ICC members and had no arrest obligation anyway.

Where the US immunity plan came to a grinding halt was with the European Union. The EU states agreed they would sign only a watered-down deal. They might give immunity to US soldiers and officials, but not all US citizens. The Bush administration then piled on the pressure. Defence secretary Donald Rumsfeld threatened to pull US military personnel out of the Nato headquarters in Brussels unless Belgium gave him a blanket immunity deal.

The EU stood its ground. It pointed out that the text of Article 98 speaks of states having the right to give immunity only to nationals 'sent' from that state. The EU said the word 'sent' meant only officials could be given immunity. The Bush administration chafed at the distinction, but backed down. In the event, EU states signed no Article 98 deals with America.

In fact, behind the growling determination of the Bush administration to oppose the ICC, even its American Service Members Protection Act is conditional. The president can send in the Marines to free American prisoners, but only if they are, the act says, service personnel. Ordinary US citizens are on their own.

The fact that the ICC even has this chink in its armour is down to the desire of its creators that it could one day be welcomed back by the UN. Remember that originally it was planned as a UN court, before too many UN members objected. Having been cast out by the UN, the ICC is like the spurned lover, forever wanting to be taken back. To this end it included Article 98 to reassure non-members that immunity from the ICC was not totally off the table. And the ICC has done more. Elsewhere in the statute, the UN has been given the power to order the ICC to investigate crimes in countries that are not ICC members. The key word here is 'order', not ask. If the UN commands it, as it has with Libya and Sudan, the ICC must agree.

A third concession to the UN is to give it the power to freeze any ICC prosecution it likes. All it needs is a vote by the UN Security Council and any ICC case can be frozen for twelve months. After which, the Security Council can renew the freeze, year after year. On the face of it, this is an outrageous rule, the worse because there is no appeal, no challenge possible. Legally, the Security Council could close down each and every ICC case it launches. Nothing in the court's statute prevents it.

The UN has never done it, but the Security Council has mulled it once. That was in 2009, when Sudan seemed on the verge of peace. One condition of a proposed peace deal was that the Security Council freeze the genocide charge against Sudan's president Omar al-Bashir. In the Security Council, four of the five permanent members were in favour of it. Britain, China, France and Russia all expressed an interest. The exception? The United States. Word came down that the Bush administration would veto the idea. America's reasoning was never spelled out, because nothing was ever put on paper. But some at the UN speculated that it was because Sudan's persecution of its Christian minority, one of many groups hammered by the regime, was a powerful cause among Republican voters.

If these chinks in the ICC armour were designed to win America over, they failed. American opposition to joining the ICC is one of the few things Democrats and Republicans agree on, though the temperature varies. Republican presidents are implacable foes of the ICC, while Democrats are polite friends. Clinton actually signed the ICC treaty, while knowing Congress would never ratify it. Then Bush cancelled that signature. Barack Obama gave public support to the ICC, while never daring to ask Congress to join it. The pendulum swung back with Donald Trump, who barred ICC chief prosecutor Fatou Bensouda from entering the country after she suggested investigating American forces for war crimes in Afghanistan. Later, Joe Biden lifted that ban. Early in the Ukraine invasion, he supported the ICC investigation, publicly declaring Vladimir Putin a war criminal. In 2022, Congress passed a law mandating aid to the ICC's Ukraine investigation. A year later, the Pentagon, presumably with support from the Biden administration – unless there had been a secret military coup – declared it would not, after all, provide intelligence to the ICC.

Among the reasons why American leaders say they cannot join the ICC is the claim that it lacks the guarantees of a fair trial normal in America. Also cited is the ICC's incompatibility with American law. The constitution says the Supreme Court is the highest legal authority in the land. So, joining the

ICC would mean allowing the ICC to overrule the Supreme Court, and to investigate Americans for crimes on American territory. By that reading, joining the ICC would be a violation of the US constitution.

Critics, notably US human rights groups, say the real reason for US opposition is to keep Americans who have committed war crimes out of jail. They point to a long list of controversial interventions, including Iraq, Panama and Grenada, as well as the fact of Guantánamo Bay. The lack of due process in the detention facility there would likely trigger an ICC investigation all by itself.

Yet the truth is that American critics are half right, because the ICC lacks some fair trial safeguards. It is the proud boast of the ICC that the innocent cannot be jailed. Prosecutors can only investigate a country if a panel of judges agrees. A second panel must agree a criminal charge, a third holds the trial and a fourth the appeal. In other words, to convict the innocent, virtually the entire judicial roster would have to be in on the conspiracy.

But, American critics point out, while The Hague can't jail the innocent, it can still detain them. Congo's vice president Jean-Pierre Bemba was held for ten years in detention in a convoluted trial process that ended with his acquittal. Laurent Gbagbo, former president of Ivory Coast, spent eight years in jail before his own acquittal. Neither man was offered compensation for their years behind bars, because the ICC does not offer reparations. Nor did the ICC explain why it took so long on these trials. Embarrassingly, Bemba's case is the longest trial in war crimes history.

And it doesn't stop there. America has three key safeguards against the state's abuse of the law: jury trials, independent, elected prosecutors, and an independent appeals process. The ICC has none of those. The ICC prosecutor, like the judges, is appointed by the states that run the court. Jury trials were considered and discarded as impractical for a court spanning two-thirds of the world. And while the ICC has an appeals panel, the judges have a conflict of interest. They know that their jobs depend on the court being successful, which it will not be if they overturn too many judgments.

US politicians also fret that the anti-American bias found in much of the world would see US citizens marked out for investigation if it joined the court. As evidence, they point to the example of another institution, the UN's Human Rights Council. Formed in 2006, the Council is the highest UN human rights body. In its first decade, it condemned Israel sixty-two times and countries from the rest of the world of fifty-five times. To Americans, that seems very one-sided.

America will likely never join the ICC, but the more the ICC moves to fix these problems, the softer American opposition will be in the future. At least, possibly. Certainly, every misstep by the ICC hardens American opposition. In that sense, America is the canary in The Hague's coal mine. The more legal fissures the ICC closes, the happier that canary will be.

The ICC could start by enacting laws that prohibit lengthy delays in bringing charges. Why it took ten years to work out that Bemba was innocent was never explained. That will need to change.

Next, it needs to be even-handed over its investigations. In Ukraine, Putin has been charged inside twelve months. By contrast, the court has been officially investigating Afghanistan for twenty years, and has never charged anyone with anything. Or explained why.

Jury trials should at least be considered. Given how many ICC states operate jury systems, there seems no reason why jurors should not be offered the option of an ICC trial. The process would be cumbersome and expensive, not least in translation services. But the court would further its claim to be acting on behalf of citizens if citizens had input into its verdicts.

Likewise, a higher judicial authority could be created, independent from The Hague. If member states deputised senior judges who also had other jobs back home, those judges would have no conflict of interest as do the present appeals judges. Monitoring could be extended to the prosecutor. The Hague prosecutor has unique powers. They, and they alone, decide who is prosecuted. It is entirely possible that a future prosecutor could indict one side in a war zone, and leave the other side free. It has never happened, but, as American critics point out, that is no guarantee it might not in the future.

All this kicks back on the ICC member states. They meet once a year, at a conference called the Assembly of States Parties. If the assembly had a permanent working group, with formal legal powers, it would mean that the ICC no longer operated as a closed system.

Prosecutors should also have to justify the increasing number of deals they have struck with states they are investigating. Karim Khan has highlighted his hope that more such deals will be made, in his eyes to speed prosecutions. Yet, prosecutors are supposed to investigate governments, not make deals with them.

It is worth noting that none of these feared violations, except for the overlong trials, have occurred in
the first twenty years of the ICC's operations. Indeed,
the appeals court has been withering in its criticism
of both judges and prosecutors in an embarrassing
number of cases. When the appeal chamber acquitted
Bemba, it savaged the original trial for convicting
him despite a yawning gap in the evidence.

But the key to war crimes justice, as with justice
everywhere, is that it must be seen to be done. If the
ICC wants to gain more public support in the future,
its masters must try harder. It will be certainly needing
such support in the near future, because it is heading
for choppy waters. The Ukraine investigation, now
so widely praised, will become an embarrassment if
years drag by with no Russian brought to the cells.

And then there is Palestine. Palestine is not
a state fully recognised by the United Nations,
which for some means it should not have the right
to request ICC investigations. The ICC itself dis-
agrees, and it accepted Palestine's request for war
crimes investigations to be carried out in 2015. It
highlighted Israeli military action in Gaza, and
settlements built on the West Bank, among things it
wanted scrutinised. Since then, it has been hard to
resist the impression that the court has dragged its

feet. It took the previous prosecutor, Bensouda, four years just to report to the judges on whether, in fact, crimes had been committed in Palestine.

Even then, no decision was reached on actually commencing prosecutions. First, the judges asked for observations as to exactly what the boundaries of Palestine were. That took another year. Bensouda finally announced that an investigation would begin in March 2021, three months before she left office. In total, six years passed between the ICC agreeing to investigate Palestine and actually starting that investigation. At a minimum, these erratic timelines need to be explained.

Now that it has started, more problems will emerge. The first is access. Israel opposes the court, and has protested the court's inclusion of Palestine in the first place. The court has accepted Palestinian borders that include territory occupied by Israel, but Israel will not give Khan's investigators access there. If Khan investigates only Israeli actions, he will face charges of bias. If he investigates Palestine too, in matters such as the launching of hundreds of unguided rockets into Israel territory, he will likely lose access in Palestinian territory also. In this most highly charged of wars, the ICC is likely to leave all sides unhappy, whatever prosecutors decide.

The other looming problem is Myanmar. Crimes by Myanmar's armed forces against hundreds of thousands of its Rohingya population are well documented. However, Myanmar is not an ICC member. When the ethnic cleansing of Rohingyas began several years ago, activists hoped the UN might authorise the ICC to investigate Myanmar anyway. No such authorisation was made. So instead, the ICC did something controversial. It opened a formal 'situation', or investigation, in neighbouring Bangladesh. Not because it felt Bangladesh had committed war crimes, but because it was hosting the bulk of Rohingya refugees in camps along its eastern border. The suffering of many of those refugees from the effects of attacks in Myanmar continues even after they reach Bangladesh and safety. So, reasoned the ICC prosecutors, in this way we can charge Myanmar's generals with war crimes.

This is tortuous reasoning. By the same token, the ICC could open dozens of Myanmar investigations in any member state, anywhere in the world, that gives sanctuary to Rohingya refugees. Their suffering most certainly continues after they cross the border, but the crimes are committed in Myanmar, not Bangladesh or elsewhere. Should a Myanmar general ever be brought to trial, their defence lawyer will likely start by pointing out that the location of the alleged crimes are outside the ICC's territorial jurisdiction. ICC rules are specific on this: a crime must have a location, and that location must be inside the border of the country concerned. For instance, Ukrainian children are being fostered illegally in Russia, but the original crime of kidnapping them originates in Ukraine. Russia may fire missiles into Ukraine from its own territory, but the damage, and the crime, happens in Ukraine.

Many, viewing the horrors perpetuated by Myanmar's dictatorship, would be happy to see the ICC bend the law. And why stop with Myanmar? The problem with that idea is that it will confirm in American eyes that the court is dangerous. Equally, ICC supporters may counter that those making the weather in America are themselves no lovers of the law. Among some on the left there is a clamour for Donald Trump to be jailed, regardless of whether he has violated any legal statute. Meanwhile, there is strong support from some on the right for Congress to be stormed and election certification halted, if voters do not vote the way they should.

And for America, read the wider world. The climate that created the ICC in the 1990s is very different to the world now. Back then, it was teeming with new democracies, most notably in Africa and South America. The future world will likely be very different. Democracy is being rolled back across the planet. Might-is-right is experiencing a renaissance. The more gloomy of ICC supporters say it won't matter much what reforms the court enacts if the world no longer wants it. Poll after poll in many democracies shows swelling support for authoritarian leaders. Many yearn not for strong law, but for strong leaders, subject only to the condition that the resulting tyranny is not turned on them.

For the ICC, the choice is stark. To have a future as a court of law, it needs to stick to the rules. The more it breaks or bends those rules the more it becomes a political, not a legal entity, losing any claim to impartiality.

Conclusion

The biggest development in the future of war crimes justice may already have happened. Almost unnoticed, in January 2023 the United States adopted the Victims of War Crimes Act. This innocuous-sounding law means that for the first time America can prosecute war crimes anywhere in the world.

The reason the law passed without fanfare is that it comes with a catch. Only the government decides who will be prosecuted. In the future, America may emerge as the boldest force in war crimes justice, or it may do nothing. The new law gives the US government the option to act, but not the obligation. That makes it a microcosm of war crimes justice. Laws are already in place, but they depend on political will. Predicting how this will go is a fool's errand. It is safer instead to sketch out the skirmish lines.

First will be whether law and war go together. It strikes many as strange that some acts on a battlefield can be labelled legal, and others see people jailed for life. War crimes is anyway a misnomer, because genocide and crimes against humanity are as likely to be committed when no formal war is happening.

And then there is the question of whether international justice should have a place in a world where the nation state reigns supreme. It is worth being pedantic on this point, because so much misinformation circulates around it. Among his criticisms of war law, Henry Kissinger argues that it conflicts with the UN Charter. And so it does. The Charter says each state can do what it likes in its own backyard. Even when it invades another state, the worst punishment available is a slap on the wrist from the UN's International Court of Justice.

So Kissinger is right. But also wrong. Because, by signing the Geneva Conventions, states forfeit some of their rights. The conventions work like a contract. You sign it, you are bound by it, including the part saying that for the worst crimes, other countries can prosecute you. Almost every country in the world,

196 in total,§ have signed. They are free to quit the conventions, but unless they do so, they allow other countries to judge them. That is the authority behind universal jurisdiction. However, while states signing the conventions promise to prosecute war crimes, few actually do it. Only about two dozen actually operate universal jurisdiction, and many, like the United States, keep it under tight political control.

Optimists say that despite its problems, war crimes justice is on an upward trajectory. They point to the rising curve starting from the first Geneva Convention and on to the Nuremberg trials, the UN courts and finally the ICC. Progress is also speeding up. The gap between Geneva and Nuremberg was eighty-four years, but there were just nine between the UN courts and the establishment of the ICC. On this metric, progress is assured.

Pessimists say the fate of the ICC tells a different story. Its return of just five war crimes convictions in twenty years has many causes, but the biggest is lack of political support. On this reading, politicians will allow war crimes justice to go so far, but no further. It may continue to operate as it does now,

---

§ This comprises 193 countries that are member states of the United Nations, plus the Holy See, the State of Palestine and the Cook Islands.

like a sniper on the battlefield: able to pick off choice targets, but not influence the wider war. The BBC's diplomatic correspondent James Robbins hit the nail on the head when he wrote: 'War criminals have some reasons to be scared of international justice, but not enough reasons to make them very afraid.'

The big political tests are coming shortly for both the ICC and universal jurisdiction. For the ICC it will be Palestine. Whatever indictments it brings, or fails to bring, in this most intractable of conflicts, it will earn powerful enemies. For universal jurisdiction, the test will be when a national prosecutor indicts someone from a major power. It is possible to imagine a Chinese official landing at a European airport and finding an arrest warrant waiting related to crimes against the Uyghurs. More than a million Uyghurs have been detained and many thousands tortured. A Pinochet-style arrest would enrage China and leave the host government to decide between politics and the law. Frustration with the shortcomings of existing war crimes courts will see new initiatives spring up. Most obviously, there may be new courts tailored to specific conflicts. The United Nations will have no role in any of this. Its Security Council, the world's most powerful arbitration body, has been blunted by Russia's Ukraine invasion. It could hardly be otherwise, given that one permanent member is invading a state being armed by three other permanent members.

Support is growing for a special tribunal to prosecute Russian officials for the crime of aggression in Ukraine. The European Union has even identified a site in The Hague. But this court will lack credibility if only Russia's enemies support it. Given that no Russian will likely surrender themselves for trial, it will probably follow the ill-fated Special Tribunal for Lebanon, which closed without anyone ever coming to trial.

More successful will be hybrid courts. Here, the affected country holds the trials, but with international help. Hybrids are already going in Bosnia, Kosovo, Senegal and now Ukraine. The Special Court for Sierra Leone showed what is possible when smart use is made of limited resources. Its managers limited prosecutions to the top leaders. Their foot soldiers were subject to a truth and reconciliation commission. Favoured by many as a painless alternative to acrimonious trials, truth and reconciliation commissions will have their place, but only to bookend wars that have already ended. As a deterrent, they are useless.

Equally problematic are initiatives to combat war crimes through education. The theory goes that if you bring warlords together, show them the error of their ways and how much they have in common, they will put away their swords. It is an attractive idea because negotiation is better than war. But it doesn't always work. In the nine wars I have reported on, ignorance was not the problem. The aggressors knew exactly what they were doing, if not how things would turn out. Early in the Bosnian war I asked a Serb paramilitary commander why he was blocking a UN food convoy trying to reach besieged Srebrenica. He thought the question strange, explaining that obviously he was doing it to starve the population. The world is not short of people willing to commit the most appalling atrocities, and only the threat of punishment will dissuade them.

In the future there will be as many war law initiatives as there are conferences and academic institutions to promote them. These will weave ever more intricate patterns, groping for a magical formula to eliminate war crimes once and for all. They will be like so many ladders, each reaching the same snake, which is the reluctance of governments to make it happen.

This book has argued that war crimes justice will work better if it makes better use of the powers it already has, notably by going after the banks and corporations that enable warlords. That one innovation, using laws already on the books, would have far-reaching consequences. In Ukraine, it would make corporations and arms traders think twice before supplying Russia's war machine. More centrally, the focus would be on future wars, which will increasingly be about the fight for scarce resources. Global corporations that finance war crimes will also be uniquely vulnerable, because they have entities in dozens of countries and could face multiple prosecutions. It will also find less opposition from politicians if it is fairer. The ICC detaining a suspect for a decade, only to find them innocent, is unconscionable.

Looming over everything is the question of whether the world of the future actually wants war law. Troubled times have come, rooted in growing populations. Poverty, migration, inequality, climate disaster and a scramble for resources may overwhelm traditional coping mechanisms. Political divides are widening and hysteria replacing reason. An unfortunate facet of human nature is that when crisis hits, rational thinking is often jettisoned, at the very time when it is needed most. In the world of the future, raw power may seem a safer bet than the law, especially to those with that power.

That being said, war law has created a momentum which makes it hard to put back in its box. The ICC continues to stutter, and may be embarrassed if Putin and his high command never appear for trial. But its problems are fixable. Universal jurisdiction continues to spread. In June 2023 Switzerland became the latest nation to finish its first ever war crimes trial, jailing a Liberian warlord.

War crimes are getting easier to investigate, and horrors harder to hide, thanks to the digital world. The best of the rights groups, including Human Rights Watch and Global Witness, will continue churning out detailed reports showing investigators where to look. The most powerful tool for war crimes justice may turn out to be the most prosaic. That is the cumulative effect of an ever-growing web of international conventions, not all related to war law. Agreements as varied as blood diamonds, conflict minerals, bribery, money laundering and terror finance will work to box in warlords and their backers.

The great, singular, achievement of war crimes trials these past thirty years has been to show that the system can work. Not always, and not always well. But it has demonstrated that vague conventions can be turned into workable laws. The concept is proven, the tool available, if the world wants to use it. The fact that an international criminal court exists at all, more by accident than design, is by itself significant. Just getting this far would likely have been considered a triumph by Henry Dunant and Franz Lieber, Raphael Lemkin and George Washington Williams.

The Facts

This book has sketched the key concepts of war law in broad strokes. Inevitably, in such a brief account, details are lost, nuance skated over. To bathe in those details, there are many fine sources for further reading.

For a concise explanation of how the ICC could prosecute corporate bosses, I recommend *Corporate War Criminals and the International Criminal Court: Blood and Profits in the Democratic Republic of Congo*. It was written in 2004 by Julia Graff, of the American University Washington Law College, but remains up to date. It is available free, online, at the Human Rights Brief portal.

For the inside story of how war crimes prosecutors work, see Richard Goldstone's *For Humanity,*

Reflections of a War Crimes Investigator (Yale University Press, 2000), along with *War Crimes and the Culture of Peace* by Louise Arbour (University of Toronto Press, 2002), a personal hero of mine. She, and Goldstone too, showed what is possible for prosecutors who know how to work the political field.

Samantha Power's *A Problem from Hell* (Harper-Collins, 2003), is a thriller-readable account of America's grappling with war crimes justice. Its account of Raphael Lemkin introduced me to one of the pioneers of war law, a man who gave it all and got so little in return. To get inside the mind of a war law pioneer, read Corinne Chaponnière's entertaining *Henry Dunant: The Man of the Red Cross* (Bloomsbury, 2022). It is an even-handed appraisal of the eccentric originator of the first Geneva Convention, and a reminder that progress, in so many fields, often depends on just this kind of maverick.

The struggle between war law advocates and reluctant governments is chronicled in *Stay the Hand of Vengeance* by Gary Bass (Princeton University Press, 2000). For the legal nuts and bolts of that struggle, see Geoffrey Robertson's *Crimes Against Humanity* (Penguin Books, 1999). Robertson explains war law like a car mechanic. He takes it apart, examines the pieces, then shows how they all fit back together.

The psychology of war criminals is examined in *War on the Mind* (Penguin Books, 1980) by Peter Watson. It is a pacy account of the dark arts of psy-ops – psychological warfare – in all its forms.

To banish the thought that war law is a recent conception, read Theodor Meron's lively *Henry's Wars and Shakespeare's Laws* (Clarendon Press Oxford, 1993). Meron, an American judge and former ICTY president, has written one of the most unusual and readable volumes in the war crimes canon, looking at how both England's Henry V, and Shakespeare's account of him, used and abused laws of chivalry.

For war law itself, three texts stand out. Top of the list, dabbling also in the philosophy behind it all, is *Cassese's International Criminal Law* (Oxford University Press, 2013). The late Antonio Cassese is regarded by many as the father of modern war crimes justice. His presidency of the first UN war crimes court set the tempo, and inspired a generation of lawyers.

Also recommended are *International Criminal Practice* by John Jones and Steven Powles (Transnational Publishers Inc, 2003), and *Archbold, International Criminal Courts* by Karim Khan, Rodney Dixon and Adrian Fulford (Sweet & Maxwell, 2018). And then there is the ICC statute. It is online and free to read, but nobody ever does. Even many journalists writing about war crimes don't read it. They think it is the law, and therefore intimidating. In fact, the statute is very readable. It was designed that way, to be understood by all, including soldiers in the field.

Further Reading

Abrams, Joseph, and Ratner, Steven, *Accountability for Human Rights Atrocities in International Law* (Oxford University Press, 2001)

Arendt, Hannah, *Eichmann in Jerusalem: A Report on the Banality of Evil* (Viking, 1963)

Best, Geoffrey, *War And Law Since 1945* (Clarendon Press, Oxford, 2002)

Doyle, Arthur Conan, *The Crime Of The Congo* (Doubleday, 1909)

Eyffinger, Arthur, *The Hague: International Centre of Justice and Peace* (Jongbloed Law Booksellers, 2003)

Gutman, Roy, and Rieff, David, *Crimes of War* (W. W. Norton and Company, 1999).

Higgins, Rosalyn, *Problems and Process: International Law and How We Use It* (Oxford University Press, 1994)

Hochschild, Adam, *King Leopold's Ghost: A Story of Greed, Terror, and Heroism in Colonial Africa* (Houghton Mifflin, 1998)

Judah, Tim, *The Serbs: History, Myth, and the Destruction of Yugoslavia* (Yale University Press, 1997)

O'Byrne, Anne, *The Genocide Paradox* (Fordham University Press, 2023)

Persico, Joseph, *Nuremberg: Infamy on Trial* (Viking, 1994)

Russell, Alec, *Prejudice and Plum Brandy* (Michael Joseph Ltd, 1993)

Russell, Bertrand, *Justice In War Time* (Open Court Publishing Company, 1916)

Sudetic, Chuck, *Blood and Vengeance: One Family's Story of the War in Bosnia* (W. W. Norton and Company, 1998)

Vulliamy, Ed, *Seasons in Hell: Understanding Bosnia's War* (St. Martin's Press, 1994)

About the Series

Each volume in the FUTURES Series presents a vision imagined by an accomplished writer and subject expert. The series seeks to publish a diverse range of voices, covering as wide-ranging a view as possible of our potential prospects. Inspired by the brilliant 'To-Day and To-Morrow' books from a century ago, we ask our authors to write in a spirit of pragmatic hope, and with a commitment to map out potential future landscapes, highlighting both beauties and dangers. We hope the books in the FUTURES Series will inspire readers to imagine what might lie ahead, to figure out how they might like the future to look, and, indeed, to think about how we might get there.

Professor Max Saunders and Dr Lisa Gee
Series originators, University of Birmingham

The FUTURES Series was originally conceived by Professor Max Saunders and Dr Lisa Gee, both of whom work at the University of Birmingham. Saunders is Interdisciplinary Professor of Modern Literature and Culture and the author of *Imagined Futures: Writing, Science, and Modernity in the To-Day and To-Morrow* book series, 1923-31 (OUP 2019), and Gee is Assistant Professor in Creative Writing and Digital Media and Research Fellow in Future Thinking.

To find out more about their Future Thinking work visit www.birmingham.ac.uk/futures

Author's Acknowledgements

I have been lucky, as a non-lawyer, to know several eminent attorneys possessed of the infinite patience necessary for me to grasp the finer points of war law. I am grateful in particular for the assistance of Mark Kersten, assistant professor of criminology and criminal justice at Canada's University of Fraser Valley, and Stephen Lamony, an expert adviser on international law. Both track war crimes developments, and following them on social media is a sure way to see the future of war law as it unfolds. Sir Geoffrey Nice KC, lead prosecutor of Slobodan Milošević, has given me much useful guidance on war law as practised at the coal face, a different reality to war law as theory. The late John Jones was both a mentor and inspiration, harshly critical of some facets of war crimes courts but also energised by their possibilities. Thanks also to Thomas Verfuss, president and stalwart of the Association of Journalists at the International Criminal Court, for much useful advice, and for powering the association forwards for so many years. Special thanks to Sadie Cambray for appraising my manuscript and offering several helpful suggestions. As with the sources mentioned in the previous section, I could not have done the book without them, but any mistakes are mine alone.

Finally, you could do worse than look at other books in the Futures series. The best way for the world to solve its problems is to think up new ways to fix them. Ideas are the ultimate silver bullet. On that note, thanks also to Nikki Griffiths, managing director of Melville House. Those deadline extensions made all the difference.